SOCIAL GRACES for Your WEDDING

ANN PLATZ ∞ SUSAN WALES

ILLUSTRATIONS BY KATHRYN ANDREWS FINCHER

HARVEST HOUSE PUBLISHERS

EUGENE, OREGON

Social Graces for Your Wedding

Text Copyright © 2002 by Susan Wales and Ann Platz
Published by Harvest House Publishers
Eugene, Oregon 97402

Library of Congress Cataloging-in-Publication Data
Platz, Ann.
   Social graces for your wedding / Ann Platz and Susan Wales ; artwork by
   Kathryn Andrews Fincher.
      p.cm.
   ISBN 0-7369-0566-9
   I. Wedding etiquette. I. Wales, Susan. II. Title.

BJ2051 .P53 2002
395.2'2—dc21   2001038501

All works of art reproduced in this book are copyrighted by Kathryn Andrews Fincher and may not be reproduced without the artist's permission. For more information regarding art prints featured in this book, please visit www.kathrynandrewsfincher.com.

Design and production by Koechel Peterson & Associates, Minneapolis, Minnesota

Harvest House Publishers has made every effort to trace the ownership of all poems and quotes. In the event of a question arising from the use of a poem or quote, we regret any error made and will be pleased to make the necessary correction in future editions of this book.

Scripture quotations are from the New King James Version of the Bible. Copyright © 1982 by Thomas Nelson, Inc. Used by permission. All rights reserved.

Printed in China

02 03 04 05 06 07 08 09 10 11 / IM / 10 9 8 7 6 5 4 3 2 1

Table of Contents

Dedication

Young *bride*, a wreath for thee of *smiles* and gentle flowers;
For wedded life was *pure* and free in Eden's *happy* bowers.
—MARTIN FARQUHAR TUPPER

This book is lovingly dedicated to our darling daughters, Megan Chrane (Susan) and Courtney Norton and Margo Cloer (Ann); and to all the brides whom God places this book into your hands to plan one of the most important days of your life . . . your wedding day.

Introduction

The social butterflies (Susan and Ann) are back again, this time with social graces for one of the most important events of your life . . . your wedding day. Just think of us as Aunt Grace—your own personal wedding advisor who will help you plan the wedding of your dreams right down to the finest details. Every bride and groom and their mothers will want Aunt Grace to hold their hand as they embark on their incredible wedding journey—from the engagement to the special day. We are also here to offer sound advice and charming etiquette suggestions for everyone involved. To insure that all the members of the wedding party will be following the same guide, a thoughtful bride-to-be will want to give copies of *Social Graces for Your Wedding* to both mothers and her maid of honor, and the groom will give a copy to his best man. If there is ever a time that you want your social graces to shine, it is on your wedding day!

God Bless,
Susan and Ann

CHAPTER ONE

Will You Marry Me?
Yes!

THE PROPOSAL AND ENGAGEMENT

Someone popped the question.
Someone said, "I do!"
—EIGHTEENTH CENTURY SAMPLER

FIRST THINGS FIRST... ADVICE TO PRINCE CHARMING

Aunt Grace suggests, "If the glass slipper fits Cinderella, then get off your knees and onto the *right* foot, Prince Charming!" Before you propose, ask her father for his daughter's hand in marriage. While this gesture may seem a bit old-fashioned to you, we can assure you that it will be returned to you tenfold where her parents are concerned. Are your knees shaking because you forgot this important step? Read on!

THE RIGHT WAY

> A heaven on *earth* . . . I have *won* by wooing thee.
> —WILLIAM SHAKESPEARE

Hunt, the son-in-law of my (Susan's) friends Kate and Bill, flew from the East Coast to the West Coast and back home the same evening to ask for their daughter Lauren's hand in marriage. Hunt obviously put a high priority on his proposal and his marriage. In his own words to Lauren's parents, "I'm only going to do this once, and I want to do it the right way." Imagine how this young man endeared himself to his future wife's parents for a lifetime!

Perhaps you have proposed without her father's permission? It is never too late to do it the right way! Visit her father to ask for his blessing on your marriage if you failed to ask him for his permission.

This is a time of great joy and celebration! It's time to tell the world that you are in love!

∼ The bridegroom's mother initiates a call to express her joy to the mother of the bride. If two weeks pass without a call from the groom's mother, the mother of the bride calls her. When distance prohibits the families from meeting prior to the wedding, the mothers become acquainted by telephone, followed by letters. The two families can get together for dinner at one of their homes, a club, or restaurant. Siblings of the couple can be included at this dinner. There are no strict rules regarding who should entertain whom, and it is acceptable for the two families to share the costs. Once this initial meeting of the parents has been accomplished, it is not necessary to reciprocate, since everyone is busy with wedding plans! Both mothers should pen a note acknowledging how lovely it was to meet and that they are looking forward to the wedding.

∼ When the out-of-town family offers to drive or fly to meet your family, you can suggest hotel accommodations; but you are under no obligation to pay their hotel expenses or to invite them to stay in your home. You can offer to pay for the dinner.

∼ It is a sweet custom to exchange small engagement gifts at this occasion. The bride and her mother can present a copy of *Social Graces for Your Wedding* to the bridegroom and his mother, inscribed with a special sentiment. The bridegroom's mother can give the bride a token of her affection such as a small picture frame with a baby picture of her fiancé or a journal for recording her thoughts throughout the engagement and wedding.

LENGTH OF ENGAGEMENT

In most cities, the length of the engagement is usually determined by the availability of the wedding and reception sites as well as the duration of the premarital counseling required. Never set the date until you have made the calls to insure availability. A proper engagement period should extend from 3-12 months. An individual who has been widowed, or who has experienced the pain of divorce, should wait for at least one year, allowing time for counseling and recovery.

THE ENGAGEMENT PARTY

I go about *murmuring*,
"I have *made* that dignified girl *commit* herself,
I have, I have," and then I *vault* over the sofa with *exultation*.
—WALTER BAGEHOT

- The bride or groom's parents, close friends of the family, or even the couple themselves may host the engagement party. If the parents reside in the same city, they can host the party jointly, or the bride's family can include the groom's family and friends on their invitation list. If the bridegroom is from another area, his parents may want to host their own engagement party to introduce their son's fiancée to their friends and family. Champagne and a cake decorated with hearts, wedding bells, or other wedding motifs are perfect for party refreshments.

- The engagement can be announced at a brunch, a large open house in the afternoon with refreshments, a cocktail party, an informal barbecue, or a seated dinner.

- The bride-to-be and her parents should greet the guests at the door and introduce the bridegroom-to-be to their friends. His parents may stand with them, or they can mingle with the guests and be introduced at the time of the formal toast.

HOW THE ENGAGEMENT IS ANNOUNCED

The father of the bride-to-be will introduce the couple, the parents of the groom-to-be, other family members including grandparents, and any special guests. He will then propose a toast to announce the engagement at dinner, or before the cake is cut, if there is no dinner.

ENGAGEMENT GIFTS FOR THE COUPLE

If you are invited to an engagement party, a small memento such as a picture frame, candlesticks, or small crystal bowl is appropriate. If your present is substantial, it can double as your wedding gift.

ENGAGEMENT PRESENT TO THE GROOM

The bride usually gives an engagement present to her fiancé, but it should not be more significant than her wedding gift to him. Along with her gift, the bride-to-be could begin a lifelong tradition of writing a letter to her fiancé, expressing her joy about their upcoming marriage.

ANNOUNCING THE ENGAGEMENT AND THE WEDDING TO THE PRESS

Call your local newspaper for guidelines and forms to announce your engagement and wedding. If the groom's family, or the bride and groom live in a separate city, make arrangements for those newspapers, too.

The bride often sits for a formal photograph to accompany the engagement announcement; and after she purchases her wedding gown, sits for a formal portrait that is used for the wedding announcement in the newspaper. In some areas, it is customary to have a photo of the couple for both the engagement and the wedding. Ask your photographer in advance to provide a photo from the wedding to meet the newspaper deadlines.

WHO ANNOUNCES THE ENGAGEMENT AND MARRIAGE

The bride's parents traditionally announce the engagement and the marriage. Examples for special situations are below:

Deceased Parents of Bride-to-Be and Groom

Mr. John David Brooks announces the engagement of his daughter, Miss Sarah Ann Brooks, to Mr. Stanley Daniel Smith, son of Mrs. Arnold Carter Smith and the late Dr. Smith. Miss Brooks is also the daughter of the late Sarah Hughes Brooks.

If the parent has remarried, the stepparent can be included: Mr. and Mrs. John David Brooks announce the engagement of his daughter. Miss Brooks is also the daughter of the late Sarah Hughes Brooks.

Divorced Father and Mother

Mrs. Kenyard Smith Wales and Mr. Robert Noland Chrane, Jr. announce the engagement of their daughter, Margarethe Ripley Chrane.

Divorce: Bride Raised by Mother and Stepfather

Mr. and Mrs. John Oliver Platz announce the engagement of Mrs. Platz's daughter, Miss Margaret Fitzgerald Cloer. Miss Cloer is also the daughter of Mr. David Henry Cloer of Jacksonville, Florida.

Divorce: Bride Raised by Father and Stepmother

Mr. and Mrs. George Stewart Collins announce the engagement of his daughter, Mary Ann Collins. Miss Collins is also the daughter of Mrs. David Bonner Atkins (if remarried) or Mrs. Carol Wright Collins (if single).

Young Widowed or Divorced Bride

Second-time brides and widows normally do not announce their engagements; only the marriage. Although the bridegroom may have been previously married, if it is the first marriage for his bride, this does not apply; therefore, both the engagement and wedding are announced.

Couples Announce Their Own Engagement and Wedding

Older couples, widows, or those marrying for a second time usually announce their own engagement although most prefer to only announce their wedding. There are couples who, for various reasons, may prefer to announce their own engagement.

Miss Carol Ann Johnson and Mr. Robert Lee Cook are pleased to announce their engagement; or Mrs. Susan Huey Chrane and Mr. Kenyard Smith Wales announce their marriage, or are pleased to announce their marriage.

Groom's Parents Announce Engagement and Wedding

On rare occasions, the groom's parents may announce the engagement if the bride's parents are ill, estranged, or live in another country.

BROKEN ENGAGEMENTS

> While nearly *every* way of *falling* in love is kind,
> Every way of *getting* out of *love* is cruel.
> J. E. BUCKROSE

Lover's quarrels are not uncommon during the engagement period so it is perfectly normal for both the bride and bridegroom to experience doubt over the upcoming nuptials. These doubts should be discussed with your pastor or premarital counselor. Despite the best intentions, some engagements are broken. However, they are far preferable to broken marriages.

A word to those who panic on the day of the wedding . . . DON'T. *Aunt Grace* insists that you get your *doubting ducks in a row* before the wedding. A bride or groom left at the altar is one of the most hurtful and humiliating experiences one can endure.

If the wedding invitations have been sent, the bride's family must notify the guests by a printed announcement, note, or telephone call if time is limited. An example is below:

> *Mr. and Mrs. John Randolph Brown*
>
> *are obliged to recall their invitations*
>
> *to the marriage of their daughter*
>
> *Elizabeth Mallory*
>
> *to*
>
> *Mr. Jason Theodore Collier*
>
> *as the marriage will not take place.*

When engagements are broken, the ring, as well as other expensive gifts from the groom or his family, must be returned. Wedding gifts should be returned with a short note of explanation:

> *Dear Mrs. Johnson,*
>
> *I regret to inform you that Michael and I have broken our engagement. Therefore, I am returning the beautiful towels that you and Mr. Johnson were so kind to send to us.*
>
> > *Sincerely,*
> >
> > *Debbie*

CHAPTER TWO

Who Pays for What?

THE WEDDING BUDGET

❧

It is astonishing how *little* one feels poverty when one *loves*.
JOHN BULWAR

Aunt Grace will help you create a memorable wedding with all the lovely ingredients no matter what your budget! What are the things that are most important to you . . . the dress, the flowers, the ceremony, or the reception? Make a list to help determine the cost of the style of the wedding you want. You can have a wedding that is simple, but elegant and memorable. Try including special traditions, customs, Scripture, vows, and poetry so that your wedding will tug at the heartstrings.

If you have a restricted budget, remember that an afternoon wedding doesn't require a meal; only cake and punch. My husband Ken and I (Susan) were married at an elegant historic hotel on the ocean at noontime, and our wedding was a third of the cost of an evening wedding.

EXPENSES

The bride's family is responsible for all wedding expenses except those that are listed below for the groom and his family, the bridal attendants, and the out-of-town guests.

EXPENSES FOR THE BRIDEGROOM AND HIS FAMILY

- ❧ Bride's engagement ring and wedding ring.

- ❧ Groom's present to the bride and gifts for his attendants.

- ❧ Boutonnieres for groom's attendants, bride's bouquet and going-away corsage, corsages for mothers, grandmothers, and stepmothers.

- The minister or rabbi's fee or donation for performing the service.

- Transportation and lodging for groom and his family, minister or rabbi, if invited by groom or his family, and lodging for groom's out-of-town attendants.

- Marriage license and blood tests.

- Transportation for the groom, the best man, and his wedding attendants to and from the ceremony and the reception.

- The rehearsal dinner site rental, invitations, flowers, food, drink, and place cards.

- Party honoring the groom's attendants, if the groom wants to host one.

EXPENSES FOR MAID OF HONOR AND BRIDAL ATTENDANTS

- Wedding attire and all accessories.

- Travel expenses to and from the city where the wedding is held.

- Cost of hosting shower or party for bride is shared among attendants. Contribution to bridal attendants' gift to bride.

- Shower and wedding gifts for the bride and bridegroom.

EXPENSES FOR USHER/GROOMSMEN

- Rental of wedding attire.

- Travel expenses to and from the city where wedding is held.

- Contribution to groom's bachelor party and gift from his attendants.

- Shower and wedding gifts for the bride and bridegroom.

EXPENSES FOR OUT-OF-TOWN GUESTS

- ❧ Transportation and lodging costs. Although out-of-town guests are responsible for these expenses, the bride's family should send them local information concerning lodging and possibly other activities in the city where the wedding will be held. If the out-of-towners are close family or friends, you may have friends or neighbors offer their homes for them, as well as the bridal attendants, since the bride's family is obligated to provide lodging for out-of-town bridal attendants.

- ❧ Cost of meals and food. Friends may offer to give a brunch or luncheon for the out-of-town guests on the day of the wedding. The couple's families often entertain close relatives, friends, and out-of-town guests following the wedding or host a gathering the day after the wedding.

EXCEPTION TO EXPENSES

There are always exceptions to the standard rules of "who pays for what," and in some areas, customs differ. In special circumstances, the families should be open to compromises or bending the traditions. To accommodate more guests or to have a more elaborate wedding, many families agree to co-host the wedding and split the costs. When this occurs, both names should appear on the invitation, but the bride's family wishes and customs are always honored.

Couples who are working often pay for their own wedding. Second-time brides and bridegrooms should pay their own wedding costs unless their families offer.

DON'T ASK

While it is appropriate to accept the bridegroom's family's offer to help with expenses, it is never proper for the bride's family to ask them for their assistance. If the bride's family cannot afford a large wedding and reception, and the groom's family does not offer to help, then the bride's family should have a small wedding they can afford.

CHAPTER THREE

Wedding Plans

PULLING IT ALL TOGETHER

⚬⚬⚬

Love always *protects*, always *trusts*,
Always *hopes*, always *perseveres*.
Love *never* fails.
1 CORINTHIANS 13:7-8 (NIV)

The first wedding plans the couple makes is to choose the style of wedding they prefer. Weddings can be small, large, simple, or elaborate. There are four styles of weddings: very formal, formal, semi-formal, and informal.

VERY FORMAL AND FORMAL WEDDING

   ❧ Number of guests . . . . .200 or more

   ❧ Location of ceremony . . . . . .Church, synagogue, large home, or garden

   ❧ Location of reception . . . . . .Club, hotel, garden, or large home

   ❧ Invitations . . . . .Traditional, engraved

   ❧ Bridal Attendants . . . . .Maid and/or Matron of honor, 3–12 bridesmaids, flower girl, ring bearer, train bearers

   ❧ Groom's Attendants . . . . . . .Best man, 1 usher for every 50 guests, or the same number as bridesmaids

SEMI-FORMAL

- **Number of Guests** . . . . .75 to 200

- **Location of Ceremony** . . . . .Church, synagogue, chapel, hotel, club, home, or garden

- **Location of Reception** . . . . . .Club, restaurant, hotel, home, or garden

- **Invitations** . . . . .Engraved or thermographed

- **Bridal Attendants** . . . . .Maid or matron of honor, 2-5 bridesmaids, flower girl, ring bearer (optional)

- **Groom's Attendants** . . . . . . .Best man, 1 usher for every 50 guests, or the same number as bridesmaids

INFORMAL

- **Number of Guests** . . . . .75 or under

- **Location of Ceremony** . . . . .Church, chapel, rectory, justice of the peace, hotel, home, restaurant, garden, beach, or park

- **Location of Reception** . . . . .Church, parlor, home, garden, restaurant, or club

- **Invitations** . . . . .Printed, handwritten, or telephoned invitations, engraved or thermographed announcements

- **Bridal Attendants** . . . . .Maid or matron of honor, flower girl and ring bearer (optional)

- **Groom's Attendants** . . . . . . .Best man, 1 usher to seat the guests

CHOOSING THE TIME OF DAY

The hour of the ceremony is dictated by the style of wedding, as well as the local customs of the area, or the church where the couple will marry.

Early Morning Weddings: An 8:00 A.M. wedding is common at Roman Catholic churches. There are also many couples who choose to get married informally: atop a mountain at sunrise, or on the beach in the early morning hours. These weddings are usually followed by a wedding breakfast.

Noon Weddings: Weddings held at high noon are often very formal, but can also be informal. A wedding breakfast or luncheon follows the noon ceremony.

Early to Midafternoon Weddings: An afternoon wedding can be semi-formal or informal. This is a great time to choose, since your reception fare can be simple . . . cake, nuts, tea sandwiches, and champagne or punch! This is also the perfect time of day for a picturesque outdoor wedding.

Late Afternoon Weddings: Late afternoon weddings at four, four-thirty, and five o'clock in the afternoon are most fashionable in the East and parts of the Midwest.

Evening Weddings: Most formal weddings occur after six o'clock in the evening, when it is proper to have candlelight. Because of the heat in the South, most formal weddings are held in the evenings.

THE GUEST LIST

First the wedding budget, next the size of the church or other wedding site, and finally the personal preference of the bride's family will determine the size of the wedding guest list. As soon as the size of the wedding is decided, the bride's mother will inform the groom's mother of the number of guests that their family can invite.

Who should be invited to the wedding? Small intimate weddings include only family members and the closest of friends. Larger weddings include family, friends, and business associates.

Many times, invitations are sent to church members and local townsfolk for the wedding service only; while separate invitations can be sent to family and close friends to include the wedding reception. These special invitations to the ceremony only, often appear in church bulletins or local newspapers. If the bride has chosen to have a small wedding, it is wise for both families to mention this to their family and friends who will not receive invitations, to avoid any hurt feelings.

CHILDREN

Depending on the wedding type and style chosen by the bride, children may be invited. It's important to most brides to include her nieces, nephews, or godchildren; or if it is a second wedding, her own children. Children whose names do not appear on an invitation are not invited, so do not embarrass the bride by calling to see if you can bring them.

THE BRIDE'S CALENDAR

Love sent me thither, *sweet*,
and brought me to *your* feet;
He *willed* that we should *meet*,
and so it was.

J. B. B. NICHOLS

Six to Twelve Months Before

❏ Schedule premarital counseling with pastor.

❏ Determine the budget with your family.

❏ Discuss hiring a wedding consultant and a secretary.

❏ Choose wedding and reception style, time and date.

❏ Decide upon number of wedding guests.

❏ Choose and reserve: wedding, reception, and rehearsal sites.

❏ *Interview and Book:* florist, caterer, cake baker, musicians for the wedding and the reception, photographer, video-grapher, and limousine.

❏ Choose attendants.

❏ Shop and order wedding attire: wedding gown, brides-maids dresses, headpieces, jewelry, undergarments, accessories, and personal trousseau.

❏ Mothers discuss styles and colors of their wedding attire.

❏ Begin compiling guest list.

❏ Register for wedding gifts.

❏ Sit for formal engagement photo.

❏ Research honeymoon destinations and make reservations.

❏ Schedule a physical exam.

Four to Six Months Before

❒ *Choose and order wedding stationery:* Invitations, enclosures, announcements and thank-you notes for before and after wedding. Hire a calligrapher.

❒ Bride and bridesmaids attend gown fittings.

❒ Choose attire for male wedding party.

❒ Finalize guest list.

❒ Order: Cake topper, place cards, napkins, matchbooks, cake boxes, favors, toasting glasses and any other decorations needed for wedding and reception.

❒ Make wedding day appointments for hair and make-up.

❒ Compile addresses for guest lists for all party hostesses.

❒ Experiment with hairstyles.

❒ Submit engagement photo with announcement to newspapers.

❒ Select and engrave wedding rings.

❒ Provide travel fares and lodging information for out-of-town guests.

Three Months Before

❐ Weigh invitations to assure proper postage and buy decorative stamps.

❐ Begin addressing invitations or give to calligrapher.

❐ Finalize arrangements with vendors: Caterer, baker, florist, musicians, photographer, videographer, and limousine company.

❐ Plan rehearsal dinner and bridesmaid's luncheon: Finalize location, date, time, menu, program, and invitations.

❐ Choose, order, and engrave gifts for attendants.

❐ Finalize honeymoon plans: Gather necessary documents (passport, tickets, and inoculations).

Two Months Before

❐ Finalize ceremony with pastor.

❐ Plan seating chart for reception.

❐ Mail wedding invitations to arrive six weeks prior to the wedding date.

❐ Address and stamp wedding announcements, and arrange for friend to mail the day of the wedding

❐ Send periodic updates via e-mail or newsletter to wedding party and families.

❐ Order wedding programs.

❐ Prepare place cards or deliver to calligrapher to complete.

❐ Mail rehearsal dinner invitations to arrive a few days after the the wedding invitations.

❐ Prepare wedding vows and toasts.

❐ Discuss financial, business and legal details: Arrange for joint bank accounts, wills, change of address and name forms. Buy floater insurance to cover gifts.

One Month Before

❏ Schedule final fittings for wedding attire.

❏ Sit for formal wedding portrait.

❏ Confirm duties with all wedding helpers: Flower pinners, pressers, decorators, personal attendants, setup crew, candle lighters, gift and guest table attendants, greeters, seaters, servers, announcers, cake cutters and anyone else.

❏ Apply for marriage license.

❏ Arrange ceremony and reception parking.

❏ Record and display wedding gifts.

❏ Write thank-you notes for shower and early wedding gifts.

Two Weeks Before

❏ Confirm all appointments and arrangements with venues and vendors, including travel reservations. Notify wedding party of rehearsal time.

☐ Determine final guest count from response cards received (call guests who have not responded). Finalize seating chart and report final guest count to caterer.

☐ Assemble and pack items to be taken to the ceremony and reception (wedding programs, favors, decorations, toasting glasses, serving pieces, etc.).

☐ Pick up wedding gown. Try it on to ensure proper fit and pressing.

☐ Bridal attendants pick up wedding attire, and try it on to ensure proper fit.

☐ Begin gathering a wedding day emergency kit (painkillers, energy bars, breath mints, bottled water, extra hosiery, needle and thread, safety pins, make-up, stain remover, and lip gloss, etc.).

One Week Before

☐ Groom and attendants pick up formal wear, and try it on to ensure proper fit.

☐ Schedule a date with your betrothed.

☐ Pack for your honeymoon.

☐ Exercise, eat well, and sleep well.

☐ Host bridesmaids' luncheon.

One Day Before

☐ Get a manicure, pedicure, and massage. Haircut for groom.

☐ Early to bed . . . sweet dreams!

Day of the Wedding

☐ Start your day with a hearty breakfast.

☐ Take a walk.

☐ Do any last-minute packing.

☐ Make time for prayer and meditation.

☐ Soak in a bubble bath.

☐ Have your hair and make-up done.

CHAPTER FOUR

What to Wear?

WEDDING ATTIRE

I choose my *wife* as she did her *wedding* gown,

Not for a fine, *glossy* surface, but such *qualities* as would wear well.

OLIVER GOLDSMITH

Choosing what to wear to a wedding depends mainly on the time of day the ceremony is planned for and in what season it will take place. *Aunt Grace* has put together this helpful chart to assist you in determining the appropriate style for your wedding attire:

FORMAL: DAYTIME AND EVENING

BRIDE

Long white or ivory wedding gown with train and veil. Opera length gloves optional.

BRIDEGROOM AND MALE MEMBERS OF BRIDAL PARTY

Daytime—Cutaway coat, striped trousers, pearl gray waistcoat, white stiff shirt, turndown collar with gray-and-black-striped four-in-hand tie or wing collar with ascot, gray gloves, black silk socks, black kid shoes.

Evening—Black tailcoat and trousers, white piqué waistcoat, starched-bosom shirt, wing collar, white bow tie, and gloves, black silk socks, black patent-leather or black kid shoes.

MOTHERS, STEPMOTHERS, GRANDMOTHERS OF THE BRIDE AND GROOM

Daytime—Long or short dresses; hat, veil, hair ornament, and gloves, optional.

Evening—Long evening gown; dressy short cocktail dress; veil, hair ornament, hat, and gloves, optional.

BRIDAL ATTENDANTS

Long dresses with dyed-to-match shoes; gloves optional.

WOMEN GUESTS

Daytime—Street-length cocktail or afternoon dresses; gloves, hat or veil optional.

Evening—Long or short dresses; veil or hair ornament, gloves optional.

MALE GUESTS

Daytime—Dark suit, conservative shirt and tie.

Evening—If women wear long dresses, tuxedos; short dresses, dark suits.

SEMIFORMAL: DAYTIME OR EVENING

BRIDE

Long white dress, short veil, no train and gloves optional.

BRIDEGROOM AND MALE MEMBERS OF THE WEDDING PARTY

Daytime—Black or charcoal sack coat with gray-striped trousers, gray waistcoat, white pleated shirt, starched turn-down collar or soft white shirt with four-in-hand-tie, gray gloves, black shoes.

Evening—Winter: black tuxedo; summer: white jacket, pleated or piqué, soft shirt, black cummerbund, black bow tie, no gloves, black patent leather or kid shoes.

BRIDAL ATTENDANTS

Long dresses with shoes dyed to match; gloves optional.

MOTHERS, STEPMOTHERS, AND GRANDMOTHERS OF THE BRIDE AND GROOM

Long or street-length dresses; gloves, head covering optional.

WOMEN GUESTS

Daytime—Short afternoon or cocktail dress; head covering optional.

Evening—Cocktail dresses; gloves, head covering, optional.

MALE GUESTS

Daytime and Evening—Dark Suits.

INFORMAL: DAYTIME AND EVENING

BRIDE

Daytime—Short afternoon dress, cocktail dress, or suit.
Evening—Long dinner dress, short cocktail dress, or suit.

BRIDEGROOM AND MALE MEMBERS OF THE WEDDING PARTY

Daytime—Winter: dark suit; summer: dark trousers with white linen jacket or white trousers with navy blue or charcoal blazer; soft shirt, conservative four-in-hand tie, white or ivory summer suit.
Evening—Tuxedo, if bride wears dinner dress; dark suit in winter; light suit in summer.

BRIDAL ATTENDANTS

Same style as bride.

MOTHERS, STEPMOTHERS, AND GRANDMOTHERS OF THE BRIDE AND GROOM

Daytime—Short afternoon or cocktail dresses, or suit.
Evening—Same length dress as the bride.

Women Guests

Daytime—Afternoon dresses, or suit, head covering, optional.
Evening—Afternoon or short cocktail dresses; gloves, head covering, optional.

Male Guests

Daytime—Dark suits; light trousers with dark blazers in summer.
Evening—Dark suits.

THE WEDDING GOWN

We agree that our prim and proper grandmothers would probably drop their china teacups with a resounding crash if they could see some of the attire that brides wear today . . . everything from miniskirts, to leather, to skydiving or scuba outfits, to bikinis, and other outlandish get-ups! The choice is yours, but our suggestions are for the more traditional bride!

The style of wedding dress you choose depends on the formality of your wedding and the season in which you marry. A bride may wear a suit or a pretty afternoon dress for an informal wedding. For semi-formal and formal weddings in the fall or winter, satin, silk taffeta, brocade, velvet and silk moiré are favorite fabrics. In the spring, lace, silk peau de soie, and taffeta are appropriate. Summer brides may choose from a variety of fabrics, including lace, cotton, piqué, marquisette, light silk, silk organdy, voile, and linen.

Once you have determined the time, date, and the degree of formality of your wedding, it is time to decide upon a wedding gown for your marriage to prince charming.

- ❧ Old-fashioned girls who love tradition may want to consider wearing your mother's or grandmother's wedding gown. Take the dress to a seamstress for estimates to have the dress fitted, updated, or restyled.

- ❧ The bride can also consider borrowing a wedding dress from a friend who is a similar size. Most former brides are happy to lend their dress to be worn again. If you do borrow a wedding gown, and if some alternations have to be made, always ask permission from the owner. If she agrees, ask if she wants the dress returned to its original state. It is best not to borrow a dress that doesn't fit properly and will require major alterations. A borrowed gown should be treated with the utmost care and returned to its owner in perfect condition, cleaned professionally. Many specialty cleaners can also pack the wedding gown in a preservation box. Show your appreciation by giving the friend who loaned you her dress a beautiful gift, such as a special piece of jewelry or a gift for her home.

❧ A great alternative to purchasing a wedding gown is to rent one from a rental establishment. While it is costly to rent a wedding gown, it costs less than buying an expensive dress that you will likely only wear once.

❧ Try perusing the vintage clothing shops, consignment shops, or specialty bridal salons for antique wedding gowns. When my (Susan's) friend, Sarah Rush, married, she was lovely in a nineteenth-century Victorian wedding gown that she had found at an estate sale.

❧ You might consider having your dress made by an established seamstress. There are many stylish patterns and exquisite fabrics available to today's bride. When my (Susan's) mother and I purchased my wedding gown, my mother who is an expert seamstress, bought yards of silk tulle to combine with some heirloom antique ivory Brussels lace for my veil. We attached the veil to an antique headpiece encrusted with jeweled beads and pearls. The veil is precious to me, and it has been worn by many brides in our family, and in our circle of friends.

❧ If you are planning to purchase your wedding gown, clip photographs of dresses you like from magazines or catalogs. Visit various wedding salons at the major department stores and wedding boutiques. Call ahead, since most wedding salons require an appointment. The budget-minded bride should check listings for wedding outlets in the area.

THE BRIDAL VEIL

Consider wearing your mother's or grandmother's veil. If you plan to wear an antique veil, take it with you when you shop to match the color of dress you buy since even the whitest of veils will turn dark with age. A veil can also be professionally dyed to match your gown.

The bride has the option of wearing a face veil. Personally, we love them! If the bride chooses to wear one, it is always short; so that the maid of honor or groom can lift the veil over the bride's head at the conclusion of the ceremony for the kiss.

A veil can be attached to a beaded and sequined caplet, a pearl encrusted headband, a pearl and jewel tiara, or a crown of flowers. A mantilla style is pinned with jeweled hairpins.

Many brides are choosing not to wear veils, and will opt for flowers in their hair. One of the loveliest brides we have seen wore her hair elegantly swept up into a twist with a pair of gardenias tucked on one side. Hats with veils are popular, and lovely wide-brimmed picture hats are an excellent choice for the bride and her attendants at an outdoor wedding.

SHOES, HOSIERY, AND GLOVES

If a short dress is worn, the bride must choose hosiery to blend with her dress. Her shoes should match her gown in fabric and color, be comfortable, and not too high, or too ornate as to distract from her dress. Shoes can be dyed to match. Never assume your feet will go unnoticed! Actress Julia Roberts discovered she had forgotten her shoes so she charmingly walked down the aisle barefoot when she married crooner, Lyle Lovett.

At formal weddings, a bride may wear short or long gloves, depending on the style of her dress. Short gloves are easily removed at the altar and passed to the maid of honor. If the bride wears elbow or opera length gloves, she can wear fingerless gloves or the under seam of the wedding finger of her glove can be unstitched, so the ring can be placed on her finger without removing her gloves.

JEWELRY

Any jewelry given to the bride by her groom should be worn. Jewelry should not distract from the dress. Pearls are a favorite choice of brides, since they are considered the most neutral jewelry. Queen Elizabeth and Jacqueline Kennedy both wore pearls on their wedding day.

BRIDAL CUSTOMS

Something *old*, Something *new*
Something *borrowed*, Something *blue*
And a *lucky* sixpence in her *shoe*.

Something old . . . It is a lovely sentiment to include family heirlooms on your wedding day. When I (Susan) married, I wore a pearl and ruby lavaliere that my grandfather gave my maternal grandmother on her wedding day. My paternal grandmother gave me a linen handkerchief she had embroidered as a young girl, to carry with my bouquet.

Something new . . . your dress and veil; or a piece of jewelry, perhaps a gift from the groom.

Something borrowed . . . ask your mother or grandmothers if they have a garter, a special handkerchief, piece of jewelry, a prayer book, or a small Bible on which you can attach your flowers. It is endearing for a bride to ask her future mother-in-law if she can wear something special of hers on the wedding day.

Something blue . . . garters usually have a touch of blue, or you can carry a white handkerchief embroidered with your initials and the date. Sapphires, or other blue stones set in jewelry, are another fine choice.

If a sixpence is too difficult to find, any other coin to wear in your shoe will do. Many brides wear a coin dated with the year of their birth.

BRIDESMAID DRESSES

The bride and her mother usually choose the style and color of the wedding attire, but the bride may solicit her attendants' opinions once the choices have been narrowed.

The bride should be sensitive to the cost of the dresses, because the bridesmaids customarily pay for their own attire. If the bride has her heart set on expensive bridesmaids' dresses, and her family can afford to provide them, she may give them to her attendants as a gift, or offer to pay for half the cost.

The bride should also choose a style that will be flattering to her attendants' body types. Consider the bodice, neckline, and length of the dress in relation to your attendants' body types. Long skirts with matching tops are excellent choices.

SHOES, HOSIERY, GLOVES, AND HAIR ACCESSORIES

The bridesmaids' shoes should be identical, comfortable, and not too high. Shoes should be dyed to match, and hosiery should be neutral so as not to distract from the dress. Short gloves are appropriate for both formal and informal weddings. Opera-length gloves look elegant for formal weddings, especially if the gowns are sleeveless or strapless. If gloves are not worn, nails should be manicured with a neutral polish.

The bridesmaids may wear hats, which are especially lovely at outdoor weddings. Other choices for hair accessories are simple bows, jeweled headbands, hair jewelry, tiaras, or a crown of flowers on their head; or a simple bloom pinned to their hair. Attendants may also choose to wear their hair up for the wedding.

JEWELRY

While many brides give jewelry to their attendants to wear, she is not obligated to buy jewelry for them. She can suggest they wear identical jewelry that is simple, such as a gold cross or pearls.

FLOWER GIRLS AND JUNIOR BRIDESMAIDS

The junior bridesmaids should wear dresses identical or close to identical to the bridesmaids' dresses, but more youthful in appearance. The flower girl's dress can be a completely different style, but should match the attendants' gowns in texture. Bows, ribbons, or diminutive floral wreaths are lovely in children's hair.

MOTHERS OF THE BRIDE AND GROOM

The bride's mother should first decide what style and color she plans to wear, and notify the groom's mother at once. Their dresses should be the same length and formality. The mother of the groom, the grandmothers, and the stepmothers should avoid wearing the same color as the bride's mother. Neither mother should wear the same color as the bridesmaids, but their dresses should blend with the wedding colors. Stepmothers and grandmothers should also be informed of the style and color the two mothers are wearing. Long dresses can be worn any time after noon. Black is an appropriate color, but *Aunt Grace* frowns on it, because it can be construed as a sign of disapproval. Save your black dress for the rehearsal dinner.

ACCESSORIES

Gloves are appropriate for formal weddings, but should be removed during the receiving line. Hats are lovely for afternoon and garden weddings, but in the evening, hair ornaments, small evening hats, or short veils are preferred.

THE BRIDEGROOM'S WEDDING PARTY

The male wedding party should all be dressed identically. For the dress code for the male wedding party, see pages 28-31. The groom and his attendants should wear black patent leather shoes. If the groom is a member in a branch of the military, he may choose to wear his dress uniform; and his attendants, who are also in the military, may wear their dress uniforms.

CHAPTER FIVE

Choosing Wedding Services

FLOWERS, PHOTOGRAPHY, MUSIC, AND CATERERS

Bring flowers, *fresh* flowers for the *bride* to wear,
They were born to *blush* in her *shining* hair.
—FELICIA DOROTHEA HEMANS

THE FLOWERS

❀ Get recommendations from friends and former brides for at least three florists.

❀ After you set the wedding date, time, color theme, and wedding attire, focus on the church and reception floral decorations, and the flowers for the bouquets, corsages and boutonnieres.

❀ First of all, check with the wedding coordinator at the church where your wedding will be held, to see what they provide. Many churches limit the flowers, and often provide flowers for the altar for a fee. They usually allow you to add pew flowers and candelabras.

❀ Begin by flipping through bridal magazines and clip pictures of appealing bouquets to take into the florist. Invite the florist to make suggestions and look at his portfolio. Fresh herbs and fruit can be mingled with flowers for an aromatic bouquet.

❀ To cut costs, choose flowers in season, hand-tied bouquets, or simple nosegays rather than elaborate bouquets.

❀ Traditional brides carry an all-white or ivory bouquet. The wedding's color theme is often carried out in the bridesmaid's bouquets.

❧ Bouquet Styles

ARM SHEAF—Long stemmed roses, calla lilies, gladioli, delphiniums, wildflowers, or lilacs tied with ribbon are carried in the crook of the bride or attendants' arms.

CASCADE—This teardrop-shaped bouquet of flowers cascades from a center grouping of flowers to fewer and smaller flowers at the bottom.

NOSEGAY—This is a small round bouquet, backed with lace, and is hand-tied with a French or satin ribbon.

POSY—A concentric circle of identical flowers hand-tied with silk or French ribbons. Each ring of flowers in a posy features a different color. Green leaves are elegant circling a posy. I (Ann) carried a posy of stephanotis, with a garland of the same flower in my hair.

SPECIALTY—Flowers can be attached to a muff, a fan, or a prayer book. When the princess bride, Grace Kelly, wed Prince Rainier of Monaco, she carried a silk prayer book overlaid with lace embroidered with pearls in the shape of a cross.

Consider the language of flowers in your bouquet:

Rose—Love

Orchid—Ecstasy

Orange Blossoms—Fertility

Lily of the Valley—Virtue

Hydrangea—Devotion

Gardenia—Grace

Heather—Passion

Violet—Faithfulness

Camellia—Contentment

Ivy—Fidelity

Stephanotis—Happiness

Lily—Innocence

Freesia—Calm

Daisy—Faith

❧ A flower used in the bride's bouquet is also used for the groom's boutonniere. The groomsmen's boutonnieres are usually made from a different flower, such as a spray of lilies of the valley, orange blossoms, or stephanotis. They can also be a single flower, such as a carnation, a white rose or rose bud, bachelor button, or cornflower. Borrowing from our European ancestors, a sprig of evergreen, which signifies *true*, can be worn with the boutonniere. Arrange to have someone available to assist the usher/groomsmen with pinning the boutonnieres.

❧ Order a going-away corsage or nosegay, or have one that can be lifted from your bouquet.

❧ Candles are used at weddings only after dark, preferably after six o'clock. Usually, two branch candelabras are placed at the altar. At larger, more formal weddings, a large tree candelabrum is placed in the center of the branches. If the church does not stock candelabras, canopies, arbors, or awnings, and you want to have them at your wedding, have your florist refer you to a rental company.

❧ If you want to have your wedding bouquet preserved, ask your florist if they provide the service, or can refer you to a company who can.

❧ Consult with the mothers, stepmothers, and grandmothers about the flowers they will wear or carry in the wedding ceremony. Many mothers are opting for small nosegays, a corsage to be pinned on their evening bag, or a wrist corsage to protect their dress.

❧ Order simple corsages for the women you invite to sit at the guest registry or gift table, or the cake cutters, and anyone who is assisting as the announcer for the receiving line. Any special guest or relative should have a corsage.

❧ Have the florist provide and decorate the basket of rose petals for the flower girl to carry.

❦ Order identical bouquets for the brides-maids and the junior bridesmaids, but request that the younger attendants' bouquets be made on a smaller scale. The maid of honor may carry a bouquet that differs slightly from the other attendants.

❦ Select flower arrangements for the reception. I (Susan) had my wedding flower arrangements transported to the reception site, which was a cost cutter.

❦ If you have a seated dinner, make sure the table arrangements are at eye level so that the guests' view is not obstructed. Use the bridesmaids' bouquets to decorate the guest or cake table, since they will not hold their bouquets in the receiving line at the reception. They should be returned to them after the reception.

❦ Arrange a payment schedule for the flowers. Most florists require a deposit, and the remainder is paid a few days before the ceremony.

❦ After the wedding, have your flowers sent to elderly family or friends who could not attend, or donate to the church.

PHOTOGRAPHER

❧ Check to find out the specification of the photos and the deadlines required by the newspapers.

❧ Acquire referrals from friends and obtain phone numbers for at least three reputable experienced wedding photographers. Interview the photographers, preview their portfolios, and obtain estimates for photography, number of prints, and the wedding album. Also, inquire if the negatives can be purchased.

❧ Once you choose the photographer, meet with him to make a list of photographs you want of your wedding. Visit the wedding site with the photographer to choose different settings for the photographs. Also choose a wedding album for your photographs.

☙ Make an appointment with a portrait photographer to have your engagement photo and formal wedding portrait taken.

☙ Appoint a trusted friend who is familiar with the wedding party, your family, and the guests to assist the photographer on the day of the wedding. This friend can point out important photo ops and special guests. Compile a photo wish list for this individual.

☙ Nowadays, many brides are having the posed pictures taken before the ceremony so that the photography does not delay the wedding reception. This is very thoughtful, but many times brides prefer not to see their bridegroom until the special moment they walk down the aisle. Make an effort to organize post-wedding photography as efficiently as possible.

☙ Some brides hire two photographers, one for candid and one for formal shots. For additional candid shots, the bride can provide throwaway cameras for her guests to capture special moments. These are collected at the end of the reception.

☙ Arrange for the photographer to provide you with proofs to select your wedding photos. Invite both families and members of the wedding party to purchase copies of the photographs.

☙ Ask your photographer to shoot some black and white photos, as well as color.

☙ Interview videographers, then select one to record your wedding ceremony and reception. Have additional copies made for close friends and family members.

☙ Today many couples put their wedding video or photos on a website so out-of-town family or friends may view the ceremony.

MUSIC

Many churches require that the bride use the organist and pianist on their staff. There is a fee for their services. Organ or chamber music is played while the guests assemble. In addition to the organ and piano, couples can include a trumpet or a brass ensemble. A trumpet, along with the organ, heralding the procession is quite majestic. A bagpipe player can also lead the wedding procession for a unique choice.

A soloist or duo perform selected wedding or love songs before the mothers are seated, and usually one or two pieces can be sung after the mothers are seated. Having choirs sing at weddings has become popular, so the church choir may be invited to sing with a soloist. Most choirs enjoy an opportunity to sing and provide the service at no charge. A small fee is appropriate for the choir director. The congregation is sometimes invited to sing a hymn as part of the wedding ceremony. The music is usually printed in the wedding program. Audition all soloists and instrumentalists for your wedding and reception before you hire them.

Enlist the organist's help in choosing the music for your wedding ceremony. The bride and groom should buy several tapes or CDs of wedding music to choose their favorites. While choosing music can be a daunting task, it is important the bride and groom participate in this selection. Not all churches will allow secular music, so make sure you check with the wedding coordinator. Many couples have music at their reception—a chamber orchestra, band, or a disc jockey to spin their favorite tunes.

CATERERS

What will you serve at your reception? The following bride faced quite a dilemma in war-torn Virginia after the Civil War, but as at most weddings and receptions, things do have a way of working out, don't they?

There should be a special dish for a wedding dinner . . . but heaven only knew where it would come from when Major

Charles Seldon married Miss James. You see rations were thin in Northern Virginia after April of 1865 at the end of the Civil War. The bride and her mother combed the smokehouse, and ransacked the cellar. "Only heaven knows where we'll get anything to eat. It looks like a choice of johnnycake with bacon or without." But heaven did know, because as the bride and groom stood in the great hall in front of the fire speaking their vows to one another, a 15-pound ham fell down the chimney and landed with a resounding crash at their feet. A miracle! It seems that the family had hung the ham to cure in the old chimney, because the smokehouse was unsafe. This one had been forgotten, and the suspending rope had frayed through just at the right time. A merry reception followed!

God smiled on this couple, but don't wait for hams to fall from heaven. Instead, plan ahead with these guidelines:

- ❧ Solicit recommendations from friends and interview several caterers.

- ❧ Decide upon the type of food service you want for the reception. When a breakfast, lunch or dinner is chosen, they are served buffet style or as a seated dinner. Stations can be set up for afternoon teas or cocktail receptions, or waiters can pass the food on trays.

- ❧ Beverages are served at bars, on trays by waiters, or at the table for seated dinners.

- ❧ Supply the caterer with the number of your guests since most charge per person.

- ❧ Schedule a taste test, sample food, and choose menu.

- ❧ Look at pictures of wedding cakes and make a selection, or have your caterer recommend a baker. More about wedding cakes on page 99.

- ❧ Make sure the caterer or the reception site carries insurance to cover the guests.

- ❧ Ask caterer to provide a box of reception food to take along on your honeymoon.

CHAPTER SIX

The Honour of Your Presence

INVITATIONS, ANNOUNCEMENTS, AND THANK-YOU NOTES

First God's *love*
And next . . . the *love* of wedded *souls*.

ELIZABETH BARRETT BROWNING

Consult with a reputable stationer to review different styles of wedding invitations, announcements, and thank-you notes. There are two types of wedding invitations: traditional and non-traditional. According to *Crane's Blue Book of Stationery* (Doubleday), the style of invitation should match the formality or informality of the event. While formal weddings are restricted to traditional invitations, there are a variety of non-traditional styles in all colors and sizes that are quite beautiful and elegant, as well as those that are simple, casual, and fun.

Traditional invitations may be engraved, thermographed, or printed in black or dark gray ink. Block or script style is used on a paneled or non-paneled quality paper stock in white or ivory. The size is $5\frac{1}{2}$ x $7\frac{1}{2}$ inches or $4\frac{1}{2}$ x $5\frac{1}{2}$ inches, with the larger size folded. Although costly, engraved invitations are preferred. The engraver will supply a thin tissue to place over the invitation. These tissues are no longer necessary to prevent smearing because engraving has improved, but they are considered elegant.

Traditional wedding invitations, and some non-traditional, are sent within two envelopes. The inner envelope is stuffed with the invitation, folded edge first or left edge for a single card. The invitation and all enclosure cards are placed in the inner envelope with the flap facing the back. The inner envelope is not sealed.

ADDRESSING THE INVITATIONS

- The wedding invitations should be weighed at the post office to insure proper postage. Purchase attractive floral stamps or love stamps for the envelopes. Invitations must be mailed four to six weeks prior to the wedding.

- A return address without abbreviations, except for numbers, should be engraved or printed on the back flap of the outside envelope. This is the address where the wedding gifts will be sent, unless otherwise noted on the gift registry.

- Guests over 18 should receive their own invitation, even if they live with their family. Children under the age of 18 are included in their parents' invitation.

- Invitations sent to a single man or woman, who is invited to bring a date, may be addressed to *Miss Susan Stafford and guest*, but it is preferable to acquire the name of Miss Stafford's escort and send a separate invitation to that individual.

- Traditional wedding invitations, and some non-traditional, are sent within two envelopes; with the outer envelope hand-addressed in black ink to the parents, and if more than one child is invited, their names appear only on the inside envelope. For example:

Inside Envelope

Mr. and Mrs. Nelson
Susan, Christopher and Jeffery

Outside Envelope

Mr. and Mrs. Gary Bradshaw Nelson
11435 Mount Holyoke Avenue
Pacific Palisades, California 90272

ENCLOSURES

There are often enclosures included in the invitations such as: *Within the Ribbon* cards that are handed to the usher and invite the guest to sit with the family; map and direction cards which guide you to the wedding and reception. Table assignment cards are for the reception. Invitations for outdoor weddings may include a rain card for an alternative location.

RESPONDING TO THE INVITATION

Most wedding invitations include a dated response card and the R.s.v.p. is left off the invitation. Fill it out, and make sure that you return it by the deadline on the card. If a card is not enclosed, you must reply to an R.s.v.p. on the lower left of the reception card or the invitation. The note should be handwritten on your finest social stationery, in blue or black ink. The envelope is addressed using the names as they appear, on the wedding invitation:

Mr. and Mrs. Kenyard Smith Wales

accept with pleasure (Acceptance)

regret that they are unable to attend (Regret)

Dr. and Mrs. Cohen's

kind invitation for Saturday,

the second of August

THANK-YOU NOTES

Thank-you notes should be ordered as soon as the engagement is announced so you can respond to any gifts. Prior to your marriage, the notes should have your maiden initials: Example: Magarethe Ripley Chrane marries John Morris Hughes **MRC or MCR,** and afterward, with your married initials, **MCH or MHC.**

WEDDING PROGRAMS

Wedding programs list the order of the service; as well as the poetry, Scripture, and prayers that are included in the ceremony, and the names of the wedding party and the participants. Some couples share their love story and may include remembrances of departed family members. Friends of the couple, children, or the ushers can hand out programs to the guests as they arrive.

WEDDING ANNOUNCEMENTS

Wedding announcements serve the purpose of informing family, friends, and business associates, who are not invited to the wedding. Receiving an announcement does not require a gift. Announcements are useful when the number of wedding guests is limited; for second marriages; when the couple has eloped; or when couples have married in a distant city or a foreign country.

Generally the same rules that apply to the invitation, apply to the announcement. Most announcements are traditional, and are sent in the bride's parents' names.

At home cards with the newlyweds' address are enclosed, or the address should appear on the lower left hand side of the announcement. This will provide an address if you desire to send a wedding present. A family friend should be asked to mail the announcements on the day of the wedding. If a couple has eloped, and the marriage is not revealed right away, only then is it appropriate to delay sending the announcements.

TOOLS OF THE TRADE

An architect has his plans, a cook has her recipe, and a bride has her card files and notebooks. When you begin planning your wedding, there are several things you need to purchase as soon as possible:

- An alphabetical card file with 3" x 5" index cards

- A calendar

❧ A wedding checklist (See pages 23-27)

❧ A loose-leaf notebook for listing gifts and responses

The file box is for your guest list. Once engaged, the bride's family determines the number of wedding guests and asks the groom's family for their guest list. You can supply the groom's family with index cards with your desired format, and ask them to prepare their list on the cards. This will save a valuable step for the bride.

How to prepare index cards to keep your wedding organized

❧ Use colored index cards: pink index cards for the bride's guests, blue index cards for the groom's guests, green index cards for members of the wedding party. Yellow index cards for wedding announcements only, white index cards for services such as caterer, church organist, etc. Keep these cards along with the wedding party in a special section, because you'll use them often.

❧ Input cards on your computer. Make a disk of the list and addresses of the wedding guests for your mother, the groom, and his mother. Print the list and give a hard copy to everyone to proofread. Place one in your gift notebook. When hostesses request guest lists, you can go into the computer file and pull the addresses you need.

❧ When the response cards arrive in the mail, keep a basket on your desk, and drop them in there immediately. At least once a day, open the responses then record them in your notebook with the number of guests in the party. Make a notation on the index card. Cross off the names of those who regret.

Nothing flatters a man as *much* as the *happiness* of his wife;
He is always *proud* of himself as the *source* of it.

—SAMUEL JOHNSON

CHAPTER SEVEN

Showering the Bride and the Groom

WEDDING GIFTS

⤜⤏

For it is in giving that we receive.

SAINT FRANCIS OF ASSISI

BRIDAL REGISTRY

As soon as a couple becomes engaged, they should register their selected dinnerware patterns and gift choices at several local stores, and at least one national chain. In making selections, the choices should cover a variety of items in all price ranges. Give as much information as possible on the registry. When asked what they would like for a wedding present, the couple or their parents should reply, "We are registered at these stores," and then name them.

BUYING A WEDDING GIFT

Once you receive a wedding invitation, you need to decide upon a gift. If you are not intimately acquainted with the bride and groom, and are only invited to the wedding and not to the reception, you are not obligated to send a gift. All family members and close friends are expected to send a gift, even if they do not attend the wedding.

When the wedding invitation is from a friend you haven't seen in years, you are not obligated to send a gift. However, if you or your family has received wedding presents from them at one time, you will want to return the favor. If you are friends of the parents, although you do not know the bride and groom, you should send a gift. The cost of the gift depends

on how close you are to the couple or their families, within the limits of what you can afford.

If you are unable to find the store where the couple has registered, call the bride or groom's mother. If you are late in buying your gift, and all the registered gifts in your price range have already been purchased, then buy a duplicate of an item, such as a stem of crystal or a salad plate. It never hurts to have extras, in case of breakage. If the bride chooses to return it, she can be credited at the store where she is registered.

Never monogram or engrave gifts, unless you know that this is an item that the bride and groom have requested on the registry, because the couple will be unable to return the items.

The question of money always arises when it comes to wedding gifts. It is proper to give a gift of money, and in some cultures, expected. An amount is never specified so you can give any amount you prefer. Stocks and bonds are also appropriate gifts.

In many communities, the checks are taken to the wedding. The bride may carry a purse that will hang on her shoulder, while standing in the receiving line, to hold the checks. A ceremonial time can also be designated near the end of the reception where the wedding guests walk up to greet the couple and give them their check.

WEDDING GIFT DELIVERY

A gift may be delivered to the home of the bride or her parents before the wedding. If you are unable to deliver your gift in person, then you can mail it, have the store send it, or bring it to the wedding ceremony. Make sure your card is well attached, and place your gift in the appropriate place.

It is proper for wedding gifts to be sent to the couple after the wedding for up to one year, although there is some disagreement with this custom. Of course, it is ideal for the gift to be sent before the wedding but if yours is late, send it with a note explaining your delay.

GIFT TABLE

In cities where people live a distance from one another, the custom of bringing the gift to the wedding ceremony and reception, is becoming more commonplace. Although this places an additional burden on the bride's family, who is responsible for keeping up with the gifts as well as transporting them, provisions must be made for these gifts. If there is room in the vestibule at the church, a gift table should be set up there, and also at the reception. At a small wedding, the ushers can take the gift and place it on the table. At the reception, guests can drop off their gift at the gift table. If the wedding is medium to large in size, we suggest that the bride appoint a special friend to receive the gifts, in order to prevent any from being misplaced or lost.

GIFTS FOR COUPLES WHO ELOPE OR LIVE TOGETHER

You have the option of sending a gift when you receive a wedding announcement where the couple has eloped. If the couple is family or a friend, we encourage sending a gift. When you receive a wedding invitation from a couple who is living together, the same guidelines for buying any wedding gift, also apply to them.

RECORDING WEDDING GIFTS

When a gift arrives, buy or prepare stickers with numbers, and assign each gift a number in the order it was received. Record the gift in your notebook, and attach stickers in the left margin. Write the number on the index card you have prepared for wedding invitation replies. If you receive a pair as a gift, use a single gift sticker for the item.

Make sure you duplicate the gift list for the groom's family. They love to see the gifts their friends and family give. They also might like to mention their appreciation of the specific gifts to the donors at the wedding, or in passing.

THANK-YOU NOTES

Thank-you notes should be sent within three months of receiving the gift. It was once believed that the bride had one full year to write her thank-you notes, but this is incorrect. All wedding and shower gifts should be acknowledged, and *Aunt Grace* recommends that you write the notes, as soon as the gift arrives, if possible. If the couple has a large wedding, or they are traveling on an extended honeymoon, *Aunt Grace* suggests that a gift acknowledgment card be sent to each donor when a gift arrives. These cards can be ordered from your wedding stationery supplier when you order the invitations.

YOUR GIFT IS NOT ACKNOWLEDGED

If three months have passed and you have not received a thank-you note for your wedding gift, you may write or call to inquire of the couple if your wedding gift was received. If more than 90 days have passed, it becomes much more difficult to trace a gift that has not arrived. Call the couple directly, not their parents. Be warm and friendly, but let them know you are concerned that they received your gift. This allows you to trace the gift through the store that sent it, the post office, or other delivery service.

DISPLAYING WEDDING GIFTS

The gifts are displayed at the bride's home on tables draped in white tablecloths or sheets. The cloths can be overlaid with tulle, bunched with bows, ribbons, silk flowers, or wedding bells. The gift boxes are tucked underneath the tables, so they can be easily moved after the wedding. The gifts should be thoughtfully arranged and categorized on the tables. It is not proper to group duplicate items that cannot be used, such as five identical teakettles. Only display one of each kind.

A lovely custom is for the bride's mother to give a trousseau tea the week before the wedding. Friends and family are invited for a delightful afternoon of tea, and a chance to view the wedding gifts and bride's trousseau.

THE TROUSSEAU

Trousseau is a French word meaning "little bundle." There are two types of wedding trousseaus—one for the bride-to-be's household and the other is for the bride to wear. In past centuries, a mother began embroidering linens for her daughter when she was born. These precious handsewn table and bed linens along with the handmade clothing were stored in a hope chest until the bride became engaged or married. The trousseau, along with the hope chest, was considered part of the bride's dowry.

My how times have changed! These charming sewing circles have been replaced with today's modern mother taking her daughter on a shopping spree for her clothing trousseau when she becomes engaged. Friends usually supply the household trousseau as shower and wedding gifts. If the bride is blessed to inherit lovely family heirlooms, she can include those with her store-bought trousseau.

Any clothing item from lingerie to wedding attire that the bride will need for her wedding, showers, festivities, and her honeymoon is a part of her trousseau. It also includes dresses, accessories, jewelry, hats, and shoes that she will need for these occasions. Lingerie showers have become quite popular. The guests will usually supply the bride with everything she needs, including her negligee and peignoir she will wear on her honeymoon, traditionally a gift from her mother at the shower.

EXCHANGING WEDDING GIFTS

It is perfectly proper for the bride to return any duplicate gifts and exchange them for something she needs. You do not have to inform the giver that you have returned their gift, unless they will be frequent visitors to your home. A bride or groom should never exchange presents from their families, unless they have their permission to do so.

WHEN A GIFT ARRIVES BROKEN

If the broken gift is sent from a reputable store, notify them at once, and the gift will be replaced. You need make no mention of this to the individual who purchased the gift for you. For gifts sent by individuals that arrive broken, examine the package to see if it is marked insured. Notify the sender at once if the package is insured, so the gift can be replaced. If it is not insured, then you must decide if you want to inform the giver that the gift arrived broken, since they may feel obligated to replace the gift. Family members or close friends should be notified immediately. *Aunt Grace* recommends that you *always* insure your gift!

RETURNING WEDDING GIFTS—BROKEN ENGAGEMENTS AND POSTPONEMENTS

Wedding gifts, along with a brief note of explanation from the bride, should be returned immediately to the giver when the wedding is canceled or the marriage is annulled. The only exception is when either the bride or bridegroom unexpectedly dies before the wedding. In this case, more time can pass before the gifts are returned.

If a wedding is postponed, due to illness or for any other reason, and there is no doubt that the ceremony will take place, the gifts may be packaged and put away until the ceremony takes place. If a wedding date has not been reset after two months, the gifts should be returned.

THE BRIDE AND GROOM'S GIFTS TO ONE ANOTHER

The bride and groom usually exchange wedding presents following the rehearsal dinner. Traditionally, the bridegroom gives his bride a beautiful piece of jewelry. The bride gives her bridegroom a lasting gift, such as a watch, a signet ring, or a pair of cuff links. While it is our belief that these gifts should be permanent, many couples also like to bestow gifts that reflect their interests.

ATTENDANTS' GIFTS

At the bridesmaid's luncheon or the rehearsal dinner, the bride may present her attendants with a gift. The value and expense of the gift depend upon the bride's resources. *Aunt Grace* recommends that the bride give her bridesmaids a piece of jewelry to wear with their wedding attire, or a remembrance engraved with the date of the wedding and the attendants' initials.

The bridegroom gives his attendants their gifts at the rehearsal dinner or at a groomsmen's luncheon or brunch. Engraved items such key rings, money clips, letter openers, cuff links, or belt buckles are popular gifts. The best man's present is usually more significant, since his duties are quite extensive. The groom can spend as much on the gifts as he can comfortably afford.

SHOWER GIFTS

Shower gifts are presented at the shower, and are not sent to the bride's home. If you cannot attend, drop the gift by the home of the hostess, or send it with a friend who is attending the affair. For extra security, place an extra card on the inside of the package.

All gifts must be opened at the shower so the donor can be properly thanked. The hostess should provide scissors for cutting, a large trash bag for the paper, and also an additional bag for paper the bride might want to keep. Appoint someone to keep a list of the gifts and the donors. Also have someone save the ribbons and bows, attaching them to a paper plate to use as faux bouquets at the wedding rehearsal.

Shower gifts need not be expensive or elaborate, but an effort should be made to ensure that they are useful and appropriate. Most showers have a theme, and you should buy your gift with the theme in mind. If you have the time and the talent, make a handmade gift. Family and members of the wedding party are invited to all the parties, so a creative gift helps with the expense.

CHAPTER EIGHT

Let the Festivities Begin!

SHOWERS, BACHELOR PARTY, AND REHEARSAL DINNER

Centuries ago a lovely young Dutch woman fell in love with a humble miller. The young woman wanted to marry the miller, but her father wanted her to marry a wealthier man, and refused to give the couple her dowry. In those days, a young man couldn't support a wife without a dowry, so the young lovers were unable to marry. The miller was a beloved member of the community who had done great kindnesses for all of his neighbors, so the townspeople took pity on the young lovers. They got together and gave the couple a shower so that they could set up housekeeping. It was told that the bride received a much larger and more impressive dowry from townspeople than the one her father was offering. Thus the tradition of the bridal shower began.

There are all types of showers: Kitchen, linen, and lingerie showers are the most popular. Today, couple showers are also popular and incorporate the interest of the couple—music, tool, gardening, bar, or library. Showers can have special themes, such as a *Round the Clock Shower* where the guests bring a gift appropriate for the time of day; or a shower where the guests bring recipes, Scriptures, photos, or poetry that are placed in a lovely keepsake book. Guests can bring pots of herbs to an herb shower. For a plant or yard shower, guests bring a clipping from their favorite plant, or a seedling from a tree for the couple's home or garden.

THE BRIDESMAIDS' LUNCHEON AND USHER / GROOMSMEN LUNCHEON OR BRUNCH

Traditional wedding parties for the bride and groom include the bridesmaids' luncheon, hosted by the bride and her mother, or given by family and friends. Family or friends can also host a luncheon or brunch for the groom and his attendants. The couple gives their attendants their gifts of appreciation at these events. But, if there is no luncheon, the gifts can be given at the rehearsal dinner, or the bachelor party.

BACHELORETTE AND BACHELOR PARTIES

The bridesmaids traditionally give a party honoring the bride. A slumber party, a spa party, or a dinner is fun and festive. Usually, this party is held weeks before the wedding—before the bride's schedule becomes too busy.

The groom is thrown a traditional bachelor party by his attendants. The best man and attendants should consult with the groom on the type of party. Make sure, if anyone plans to do something a little outrageous, that you let the bride and groom know, so they have the option to stop it.

Choose a location for the party: a home, a restaurant or a club. My (Susan's) husband recently attended a bachelor party for a groom who was a baseball fan, and the group attended a ballgame together. There are many options for bachelor parties. Only the groom's wedding party, close friends, and family members in the age group are invited to attend. The bride's father or her relatives are usually not included, unless they are close friends of the groom.

Invitations may be sent or phoned, and should include date, time, place and attire. A response is required. It is also thoughtful to include directions to the party, including the phone number of the party site and parking logistics.

Even if some of the members of the wedding party plan to arrive at the last minute, it is better to exclude them, than to risk having the party the night before the wedding.

THE REHEARSAL DINNER

The bridegroom's parents can host the rehearsal dinner in their home, a restaurant, or a special site for parties. If the wedding takes place somewhere other than their hometown, the bride's parents may be asked to recommend a location. Check with the chamber of commerce for some suggestions.

CHECKLIST FOR THE GROOM'S PARENTS FOR REHEARSAL DINNER

- ❧ Decide upon the style and location of your party. You can have a family-style or formal dinner. For large groups, host an informal gathering: beach party, picnic, harvest hoedown, or backyard barbecue.

- ❧ Choose a menu with a special dessert, and sparkling cider or champagne, for toasts.

- ❧ Order flowers from a local florist, or ask the facility if they provide flowers. Provide candles for a candlelight dinner.

- ❧ Choose a color theme for flowers and decorations. Photos of the bride and groom, from childhood to the present, as well as family photos, can be grouped with the flowers in the center of the tables.

- Have a photo shop compile selected photographs of the couple with background music of their favorite songs for a video to be shown at the dinner.

- Make a guest list. It is customary to invite the members of the wedding party and their spouses, the clergy and his spouse, the parents of child wedding attendants, the parents, grandparents, and immediate family members of the couple, who are not in the wedding party, and out-of-town wedding guests.

- Order the invitations with date, time, and dress code. Coordinate mailing the rehearsal dinner invitations to arrive within days of the wedding invitations.

- There is always a bride's table at the rehearsal dinner. (See seating arrangements on page 97 for seated dinners.) A seating chart and place cards should be made for all the tables.

- Visit the site on the day of the dinner to arrange the place cards, check the room, and take care of any last-minute details.

- Arrive early to welcome all the guests warmly and make sure the party ends at a reasonable hour, to allow a good night's sleep for the wedding party.

The minute I *heard* my first love *story*
I started *looking* for you,
Not *knowing* how blind that was.
Lovers don't *finally* meet somewhere.
They're in each *other* all along.

—RUMI

CHAPTER NINE

The Wedding Party

WHO DOES WHAT?

❧

I have *read* those absurd *fairy* tales in my time,
but I never, never, never *expected*
to be the *hero* of a romance in real *life*
as *unlooked* for and unexpected as the *wildest* of them.

—MARK TWAIN

THE BRIDE AND BRIDEGROOM

All the months of planning are behind you, and the big day has arrived! You have absolutely nothing to do but smile, look beautiful or handsome, and radiate joy, peace and love. Arrive at the ceremony on time, recite your vows, greet the guests in the receiving line, cut the cake, toss the bouquet and the garter—then go on your honeymoon! Today is your day!

PARENTS OF THE BRIDE

For I that *danced* her on my knee,
that watched her on her *nurse's* arm,

That *shielded* all her life from harm,
at last must part with *her* to thee.

—ALFRED, LORD TENNYSON

If you've seen the movie by the same name, you know that the father of the bride usually has only three major functions . . . to write the checks, give the bride away, along with the mother of the bride, and host the reception. The mother of the bride should have no duties at the wedding, only to enjoy the ceremony and provide emotional support for her daughter. The wedding coordinator, or a trusted friend, should handle all the details of the day so she can remain at her daughter's side.

At the reception, the mother and father of the bride stand in the receiving line, and are the first to greet the guests. Afterward, they mingle with the guests, or sit at the parents' table. Stepparents may stand in the line if their names appear on the invitation.

PARENTS OF THE BRIDEGROOM

There's an old piece of advice for the mother of the bridegroom that has circulated around for years, "Wear beige and keep quiet." Sounds rather harsh, but the mother of the bridegroom has a minor role and should relax and enjoy the wedding.

If the father is the best man, refer to the duties below; otherwise, he will follow the usher seating his wife, and sit with her. At the reception, the father of the groom mingles with the guests, unless he is invited to stand in the receiving line with his wife.

BRIDESMAIDS

A happy *bridesmaid* makes a happy *bride*.

—ALFRED, LORD TENNYSON

A bride may select 1 to 12 attendants, with the average wedding having 3 to 6, plus the maid or matron of honor. Also consider the size of your church and the area where the attendants will stand. Remember, the more bridesmaids, the more expenses you will incur. If you have a large number of friends, but want to limit the size of your wedding, ask them to perform other duties, such as a reading during the ceremony. They can also preside at the guest registry, the gift table, cutting the cake, handing out favors, or greeting guests at the reception.

Bridal attendants may be married or single and any age. With the exception of the matron of honor, married attendants are bridesmaids, not bride's matrons. Bridesmaids, ages 8 to 14, are considered junior bridesmaids. While these young girls are included in the rehearsal, the wedding, and reception festivities, you are not obligated to include them at every wedding party or shower.

The bridesmaid's duties, similar to the maid of honor's, are listed below:

MAID OR MATRON OF HONOR

Bells are *ringing*, birds are *singing*,
All the *world* is glad and gay;
We are *waiting* with our *posies* of the sweetest *scented* roses
On our sister's *wedding* day!

—GITHA SOWERBY

No matter how small the wedding, the bride always chooses a maid or matron of honor or both since there must be at least one attendant to sign the marriage license and one to assist the bride in many other ways. We like to think of the honor attendant as a lady-in-waiting who attends to her queen! The honor attendant should be organized, cool, calm, and collected to help take pressure away from the bride on the day of the wedding.

The bride chooses the person closest to her, usually a sister or close friend, for the position of maid and/or matron of honor. A maid is a single woman; a matron is married. If the bride has two sisters, single and married, it is an ideal solution to choose both. If the bride does choose both, the two attendants may share the duties, or the bride may appoint one of them as the key attendant who stands next to the bride.

CHECKLIST FOR BRIDESMAIDS AND MAID OF HONOR—♥♥ MAID OF HONOR ONLY—♥

Pre-Wedding

♥ *Be a lady-in-waiting*
Throughout the wedding festivities, ceremony, and reception, the honor attendant assists and acts as advisor and helper to the bride.

♥♥ *What's a girl to wear?*
Attend the dress fittings. Savvy bridesmaids make a festive occasion out of this task and arrange for tea or lunch to fellowship with the bride.

♥ ♥ *Pen pal*

Offer assistance in addressing the wedding invitations and announcements. If your handwriting is not the best, you can always help stuff and stamp.

♥ ♥ *Party girl*

Attend as many of the parties and showers as you can in honor of the bride and the groom. This can be quite expensive if the bride is feted with parties galore, so be creative with your gift ideas.

♥ *The hostess with the mostess*

The honor attendant organizes the bridesmaids and plans a party for the bride. This can be a luncheon shower, or tea, or any other festivity that you think the bride might enjoy. The maid or matron of honor will also take up money, and together with the bridesmaids, choose a special gift for the bride.

Rehearsal Dinner

♥ ♥ *The bridal table*

The maid of honor sits to the left of the bridegroom, with her escort seated to her left.

♥ ♥ *Raise your glass*

The maid of honor may propose a toast and make a little speech in honor of the bride and groom. If you don't have a problem speaking in front of a crowd, this is a lovely gesture. After the maid of honor, any or all the bridesmaids may make a toast and say a few words.

♥ ♥ *Chaperone the junior bridesmaids*

The maid of honor should appoint one of the bridesmaids to look after the needs of the junior bridesmaid(s), flower girls, and any other children members of the wedding party, throughout the wedding rehearsal and ceremony.

The Wedding Day

♥ *Dressed to the nines*

A bridal director and the mother of the bride often help the bride dress for the ceremony, but the maid of honor can also assist.

♥ ♥ *Here comes the bride!*

The bridesmaids walk in front of the maid of honor. Their order can be arranged by height with the tallest first, unless the maid of honor is tall, then the shortest attendant will go first. The maid of honor always walks just in front of the bride in the processional, and just behind the bride in the recessional, with the bridesmaids following. If there are flower girls and ring bearers, the attendants walk ahead of the children (processional), and behind them (recessional). If there are two honor attendants, the maid of honor is usually the one beside the bride; however, if the matron is a close sister or friend, it is perfectly acceptable to reverse these two positions.

♥ *Flower focus*

The maid of honor holds the bride's flowers during the ring ceremony, as well as her own. If the bride's bouquet is quite large, she may hand her own flowers to the bridesmaid to her left.

♥ *Rings on her fingers*

If the best man or ring bearer doesn't carry both wedding rings, the honor attendant holds the groom's ring for the bride, and presents it to the minister at the appropriate time during the ceremony.

♥ *Just one kiss!*

When the minister pronounces the couple man and wife, he then instructs the bridegroom that he may kiss the bride. The maid of honor assists the groom in lifting the veil. After the kiss, the maid of honor returns the bride's flowers to her, then adjusts the train and veil before the bride turns to walk back up the aisle.

♥ *Legal matters*

The maid of honor signs the marriage license as the bride's witness.

Reception

♥♥ *Receiving line and bridal table*

The maid of honor stands to the left of the newlyweds, next to the groom in the receiving line. She then sits to the groom's left at the bridal table. The bridesmaids are seated at nearby tables with their husbands, escorts, or an available usher/groomsman.

♥♥ *A toast to the happy couple*

The maid of honor and the bridesmaids have the option to toast the newlyweds at both the rehearsal dinner and the wedding reception. Provide a copy of the toast to the bride for her bride's book.

♥♥ *Always a bridesmaid?*

The maid of honor gathers the single bridesmaids to catch the bouquet.

♥♥ *I could have danced all night . . .*

The maid of honor dances her first dance with the bridegroom, and then the best man. The bridesmaids may join the dancing floor after the maid of honor's dance with the best man. Bridesmaids should dance their first dance with the usher who escorted them, and their next dance with their date.

♥ ♥ *Farewell*

The maid of honor, often accompanied by the other bridesmaids, escorts the bride to the dressing room, to assist her in dressing for her honeymoon. Go over a mini-checklist with the bride as she finishes dressing. Send a bridesmaid to fetch any forgotten items. Summon the bride's parents for their farewell to their daughter before she leaves on her honeymoon. While she is enjoying a private moment with her family, call the best man to carry the remainder of her luggage to the getaway car. Give him the estimated time the bride will be ready.

♥ ♥ *The Getaway*

The maid of honor gathers the bridesmaids together for the bride's departure and sees the bride off. Shower the happy couple with bubbles, rose petals, or birdseed.

Post Ceremony

♥ *The party's over*

The maid of honor makes a final inspection, to assure nothing of the bride's is left behind. Offer to help the bride's parents in any way. Help carry the wedding gown and any belongings to their car following the bride's departure.

♥ ♥ Write a note of thanks to the bride and her parents for including you in the wedding.

JUNIOR BRIDESMAIDS

Too young to be a bridesmaid? Too old to be a flower girl? The bride and groom often have younger siblings, nieces, and children of their closest friends whom they want to include in the wedding. It is a joy for young girls from ages 8 to 14 to be junior bridesmaids. Junior attendants must attend the rehearsal, but they are often too young to attend many of the other parties.

FLOWER GIRLS

This tiny attendant is between the ages of three and seven years old, and her job is to scatter rose petals in the bride's path. The flower girl walks behind the maid of honor, and ahead of or with the ring bearer before the bride, in the wedding processional.

Often a bride will choose more than one flower girl if there are several young family members the bride wishes to include in her wedding. These flower girls are usually family members of the bride and groom, or perhaps the daughter of a close friend.

Flower girls and their parents attend the rehearsal, and can attend the rehearsal dinner—depending on their age. They can also be included in some of the parties, if appropriate.

RING BEARERS

Ring bearers are the same age as flower girls—ages three to seven. These attendants are family members, children from previous marriages, or children of close family friends. Ring bearers dress in the same attire as the usher-groomsmen.

The ring bearer carries a small satin, lace, or velvet pillow with the rings attached by a single thread; however, most brides are opting for these tiny tots to carry fake rings.

The ring bearer walks directly in front of the bride, and behind or with the flower girl in the processional. In the recessional, he holds hands with the flower girl following the newlyweds, with the maid of honor and the best man behind to guide them on their descent.

The ring bearer attends the rehearsal and the rehearsal dinner with his parents.

TRAINBEARERS OR PAGES

If a bride has a large train on her dress, as well as young male family members who she would like to include in her wedding, she can select trainbearers to carry her train. The young boys dress like the ring bearer. Their responsibility is to hold the back of the train, guiding it down the aisle. Other young boys can be pages, whose only duty is to walk in the processional ahead of the flower girl and the ring bearer.

CANDLELIGHTERS

If there are wedding tapers to light at the altar, appoint two candlelighters or acolytes. This will be done at the beginning of the service, after the aisle cloth is rolled down. They walk two by two, and they light the candles. Have a step stool available.

BEST MAN

It is a great honor, as well as a great responsibility, to be chosen as the best man. Before the groom chooses the best man or a best man accepts the position, all the following duties should be considered. This is a post for a responsible, organized, and dependable individual. The most important function of the best man is to relieve the bridegroom of as many duties as possible.

The bridegroom may choose his father, his closest brother, or his best friend as his best man. Many times the groom will appoint his father as an honorary best man, and then choose a friend who performs the duties. In second marriages, where the groom has older children, he will often ask his son to be the best man.

CHECKLIST FOR THE BEST MAN AND USHER/GROOMSMEN

Two Months Before the Wedding

- *Help plan fittings for wedding attire*
  Often the bride and her mother will choose the attire for the male members of the wedding party, along with the

groom. Many times the groom will ask his father and/or best man to share their opinions.

Offer to call the groomsmen and suggest a time for them to be measured for their wedding attire a month before the wedding. If they have schedule conflicts, give them the information to make their own arrangements. Volunteer to send out-of-towners the information, ask them to be measured, and have them send their measurements to you. After everyone has been measured, call the store to confirm so that no orders will be lost. If there are any male children in the wedding party, it is important to note this, since smaller sizes are limited.

People often change sizes, so make a fitting appointment no sooner or later than one month prior to the wedding. Suggest to the groom to have breakfast, lunch, or dinner before or after. The best man should have everyone's phone, pager, and cell-phone numbers available, in case anyone runs late or does not show up.

One month before

● *Meet the groom at the church to discuss the logistics*

The best man often supervises the seating on the day of the wedding, or he appoints a head usher because he is often busy with the groom.

● *Plan the bachelor party*

The best man should consult the groomsmen to plan the bachelor party. Often the wedding party will share the cost of the party, with the best man acting as the lead host, making the arrangements.

● *Gift for the bridegroom*

The best man contacts each usher/groomsman to discuss a personal gift for the groom from the wedding party. Once a decision has been made as to the gift and the cost, the best man collects the money, purchases the gift, and has it wrapped. The best man presents the gift to the groom on behalf of the wedding party, usually at the rehearsal dinner. If there is a brunch or luncheon honoring the groom, where he presents his gift to his attendants, then the best man will present the gift at that time. There are a variety of gifts appropriate for the groom. Most wedding parties like to choose a memento engraved with the date of the wedding. Some popular gifts are a silver frame to hold a photo of the wedding party, a letter opener and desk set, a crystal decanter, a piece of luggage, two tickets to his favorite concert or sporting event, or a gift certificate for a special restaurant.

Week of the Wedding

❧ Host the bachelor party

Confirm the reservations. Arrive at least half an hour before the party is scheduled to check all the arrangements. During dinner, offer a toast to the groom that includes what a good friend he has been, and recall the special times you have shared. Ask the other guests to do the same.

❧ Final fitting

Arrange for the male wedding party to pick up their rented attire. It is best for each individual to go to the rental store for a final fitting to avoid any problems, especially for those members who sent their measurements. The best man should pick up any attire for the individuals who haven't arrived in town, or who are unable to pick up their own. Make sure it is delivered to them or to the church.

❧ Help the groom get ready for wedding and honeymoon

The best man helps the groom pack and takes his suitcase to the church. Make sure the groom's attire is pressed and is delivered to the church or to his home. He returns his wedding attire and the groom's to the rental site, and makes sure all the other attendants return theirs.

❧ Confirm honeymoon reservations and details

Confirm arrangements for limo or getaway car, and always check the gas. Call the hotel for the groom to confirm the reservations. Verify flight reservations and make a note of any last-minute flight changes.

Rehearsal

◆ *Appoint an usher to oversee young attendants*

Ask one or more of the ushers, depending on the number of children, to be a big brother to the ring bearers, junior ushers, and any other male children in the wedding party. This usher should keep an eye on the younger set, and guide them throughout the rehearsal.

The Wedding Day

◆ *Get him to the church on time!*

It is the best man's responsibility to get the groom and the usher/groomsmen to the church at the appointed time, one to two hours before the ceremony. The stories we've heard about tardy bridegrooms would curl your bride's wedding veil! Be a good best man, and make sure your bridegroom doesn't leave the bride waiting at the altar!

◆ *Help the bridegroom get dressed for the ceremony*

If he needs assistance dressing, help him with his tie, suspenders, or anything else he might need before the wedding. Make sure he is properly groomed. Take along a little emergency kit with needle and thread, extra buttons, breath mints, extra cash, hair spray, comb and brush, spot remover, extra toothbrush, mouthwash, lotion, and pain relievers. It is a good idea to provide a case of bottled water and healthy snacks to have at the church for the wedding party.

◆ *Wedding party inspection*

Check with each member of the wedding party to make sure they are fully dressed and nothing has been forgotten. Double check that everyone has a boutonniere and it is pinned on properly.

◆ *Stay with "this ring"*

The best man should keep the wedding ring in his pocket, or if it fits, on a finger.

◆ *Last-minute details*

Gather ushers, groomsmen, and other male members of

the wedding party to go over duties, ask questions, and check details. Make sure everyone knows their position and their duties. Remind the ushers that have been chosen or assigned to escort the mothers, grandmothers, and great grandmothers of the bride and bridegroom.

The Ceremony

❧ *Entry and exit to the church*

At Christian weddings, the best man enters the sanctuary with the groom and the clergy, usually from a side entrance. In Jewish and some formal weddings, the best man precedes the groom in the actual wedding procession. At the recessional, the best man escorts the maid or matron of honor down the aisle, behind the bride and groom.

❧ *The rings please!*

The best man should have the rings ready to give the minister when he asks for them. If the rings are on the ring bearer's pillow, he will hold the pillow up for you to retrieve the rings for the minister.

Following the Ceremony

❧ *Marriage license and clergy's fee*

The best man signs the marriage license, along with the bride, groom, maid of honor, and minister, following the ceremony. At the same time, he delivers the groom's check for the minister, or gives cash to the clergyman for his services. Oftentimes, if the minister is the bride's family pastor, the family will make an additional contribution.

❧ *Gather the wedding party for photos*

Help the wedding director round up the wedding party and the families for post-ceremony photographs.

❧ *Help the wedding party get to the reception*

> If the reception is planned off-site, make sure all the members of the wedding party have transportation. Help bridesmaids into their cars. If there is not a chauffeur, you may be asked to drive the bride and groom.

Wedding Reception

❧ *Receiving line*

> The best man never stands in the receiving line, but it is his responsibility to mingle with the guests. He should offer to help the bride's family in any way he can at the reception.

❧ *Bridal table*

> If there is a bridal table, the best man sits to the right of the bride.

❧ *Toastmaster*

> The best man initiates the first toast to the newlyweds. He also reads any telegrams and messages sent to the couple, then saves them to give to the couple later.

❧ *Dancing Details*

> After the bride has her first dance with her groom, her father and her father-in-law, it's now the best man's turn to invite her to dance. The best man dances with the mother of the bride, the mother of the groom, then the maid of honor, and after that, each of the bridesmaids.

❧ *Help the groom prepare for his honeymoon departure*

> Signal the groom at the pre-arranged time, for the couple to dress for their departure. Escort him to the dressing room. Coordinate the newlywed's time of departure and meeting place with the maid of honor. Go over a checklist with the groom to make sure he has his tickets, wallet, personal phone book, money, and credit cards.

If he is driving, make sure he has his car keys and a full tank of gas.

Locate the mother and father of the bridegroom, and escort them to the dressing room to bid their son farewell. While they are saying their farewells, transfer the groom's and bride's luggage and belongings to the trunk of the getaway car or limo.

❧ *Ready for the getaway*
Arrange for the limo driver or the groom's car to be driven around to the entrance where the couple will leave. Many times the best man will drive the couple to the airport and safely return their car to the groom's family. Or, the best man will drive the couple in his own car.

❧ *Mr. Clean-up detail*
As the newlyweds' car disappears into the sunset, return to the celebration. When the guests depart, take a stroll through the reception site and the dressing rooms to make sure no personal items were left behind. Round up all the tuxes and other clothing left in your charge, and return them to the rental store.

❧ *Give thanks*
Express your gratitude to the parents of the couple, and ask if there is anything else you can do. Celebrate a job well done if you have followed these suggestions!

❧ *Final duties*
Write a thank-you note to the parents of the bride for the wedding and reception, and to the parents of the groom for the rehearsal dinner. Write a note of congratulations to the bride and groom, and thank them for including you in the wedding party.

USHER / GROOMSMEN

Usually there are as many usher/groomsmen as brides-maids; however, the groom should have a minimum of two ushers for 50 or fewer guests. An additional usher should be added for every 50 guests. The ushers also function as the groomsmen, standing with the groom during the ceremony, and escorting the bridesmaids in the processional. On rare occasions, for large, ultra-formal weddings, groomsmen can be chosen in addition to the ushers. In this case, the ushers will seat the guests, and the groomsmen will participate in the ceremony. If separate groomsmen are chosen, the only function of the ushers is to seat guests. Throughout the service, the ushers will remain at the back of the church.

DUTIES OF THE USHER / GROOMSMEN

Prior to the Wedding

❧ *Fittings for wedding attire*

Each usher should be fitted by a certain date for his tuxedo and pays for the cost of his wedding attire. It is wise to try on the attire prior to the wedding day, to check the fit.

❧ *The bachelor party*

The ushers should help the best man plan the bachelor party. They should also contribute money to buy a joint gift for the bridegroom.

❧ *Rehearsal*

All the ushers should attend the rehearsal and the rehearsal dinner, promptly. Arrange for the bride and bridegroom to provide a typed list of special seating assignments and to designate special pews at the church, so ushers can accommodate their wishes. Discuss plans for elderly or special needs guests. Check the handicap access and ramps to the church.

At the rehearsal dinner, each usher should deliver a toast to the bride and groom.

The Wedding Day

❧ *Arrival*

All the ushers should arrive at least one to two hours before the ceremony, depending on the time assigned by the wedding coordinator or the bride's mother. If you are not given a time at the rehearsal, make sure you ask.

Getting ready

To avoid wrinkles, take your clothes to the church and get dressed there. Have someone, usually from the florist, pin your boutonniere onto your lapel.

Seating the wedding guests

The ushers should stand at the door of the church or other ceremony site ready to escort the female guests. Welcome each arriving guest with a smile, brief greeting, and hand them a wedding program. For larger weddings, it is wise to appoint one usher to remain at the church entrance as the official greeter and troubleshooter.

When the seating usher approaches a female guest, he should first ask if she is a friend of the bride or the groom, and seat her accordingly. The bride's guests are seated on the left side of the church, and the groom's on the right side. In cases where there are few guests on one side, mix the guests on both sides.

All female guests, other than babes in arm, regardless of age, are ushered to their seats. The usher offers his right arm to each arriving female guest. If there is more than one female guest in the arriving party, another usher steps up for each additional female. The guest is escorted down the aisle to her seat with her escort following behind along with any additional male guests in the group, including male children. When the usher seats the guest, he stands aside to allow her escort(s) to enter.

If a group of male guests arrives without female escorts, the usher should ask them if they are friends of the bride or groom, and lead them to their seats. If a solitary male arrives, the usher should walk beside him to his seat.

Often when a large group of guests arrives simultaneously, an usher may escort two ladies on each arm, or the male escort may take his companion's arm, and the usher can lead several couples at once to their seats.

Guests bearing gifts

If there is ample space, a gift table should be set up inside the church entrance. For smaller weddings, the ushers should direct the guests who arrive with a gift to the gift table. If there is no room for a table, the usher should take the gifts to a designated area.

❧ *Seating the mothers and grandmothers*

Designated ushers will seat the mothers, stepmothers, and grandmothers of the bride and bridegroom. (See details on page 88.) Special ushers such as sons, grandsons, nephews, or special friends are chosen for the honor of seating family members. If the mothers are lighting the unity candle, the ushers return to escort them simultaneously to the candle, or they may each light their candles before they are seated.

❧ *Late arrivals*

Late arrivals will be directed to quietly slip into back pews, since the ushers seat no one after the mothers have been seated.

Reception

❧ *Receiving line*

The ushers will mingle with the guests instead of standing in the receiving line.

❧ *The garter*

When the bridegroom ceremoniously tosses his bride's garter, all the single usher/groomsmen gather round to catch it.

❧ *The Getaway Car*

The usher/groomsmen should supervise and assist in decorating the getaway car.

❧ *Final Duties*

After the newlyweds' departure, offer your assistance to the best man and the families. There are often guests who need assistance. Make sure you return your wedding attire to the store within the time limit. Write a thank-you note to the parents of the bride for the wedding and reception, and the parents of the groom for the rehearsal dinner. Write a note of congratulations to the bride and groom, and thank them for including you in the wedding party.

JUNIOR USHER / GROOMSMEN

These youthful attendants are dressed in the same attire as the ushers. Unless needed, these young ushers do not seat the guests. However, it is fun for a young girl to be ushered down the aisle by someone close to her own age and size. The junior usher/groomsman's main duty is to roll the bridal carpet or aisle cloth down the aisle, just before the procession. Junior attendants also attend the rehearsal and dinner.

CHAPTER TEN

With This Ring
I Thee Wed

THE WEDDING CEREMONY

Bone of my *bones*, and flesh of my *flesh*.
—GENESIS 2:23 (KJV)

PROMPT ARRIVAL

Ideally, wedding guests should arrive at the church approximately 15 minutes before the ceremony is slated to begin. For larger weddings, guests should arrive 30 minutes early. Members of the wedding party are instructed to arrive one to two hours before the ceremony.

Enter the church, and wait for an usher to seat you. He will inquire if you are a friend of the bride or groom. If a pew card is enclosed in the invitation, present it to the usher. If not, inform the usher if you are a relative of the bride or groom, and he will seat you within a reserved family section.

DIDN'T GET TO THE CHURCH ON TIME?

If you arrive after the bride's mother has been seated, slip quietly into a back pew. When you arrive and the wedding party is congregated in the vestibule, wait outside or enter the church through a side door. Should you arrive after the service has begun, you can sit in a back pew, as long as it is not during a prayer. If there are no seats, stand at the back and side of the church.

To everything there is a *season*,
and a time to every *purpose* under heaven.
ECCLESIASTES 3:1 (KJV)

SEATING THE MOTHERS

The groom's family is seated on the right side and the bride's family on the left. The grandmothers and the mother of the bridegroom are seated approximately seven to ten minutes before the service is scheduled to begin. The mother of the bride is seated last, five minutes prior. The mothers occupy the first pew. If the groom's father is not the best man, he will follow his wife and sit beside her. Once the mothers are seated, no more guests are seated by the ushers.

In today's world, there are often stepparents to be considered. The bride's mother and stepfather are seated in the first pew. Any step siblings are seated in the second pew. The rest of the bride's mother's family is seated behind. The father of the bride would then be seated with his wife behind them. If everyone is amicable, they may all be seated on the first pew. The same applies to the groom's family.

AISLE CLOTH

If an aisle cloth is used, two ushers or junior ushers roll the cloth up the aisle after the mothers are seated and before the processional begins.

THE UNITY CANDLE

A unity candle signifies two lives and two families becoming one. It is a large center candle, flanked by tapers that represent the two families. Before they are seated, the mothers of the couple are escorted up to light the tapers, then they take their seats. During or at the end of the ceremony, the bride and groom take their mothers' lit candles, and together, they light the center candle.

THE RINGING OF BELLS

> Hear the *mellow* wedding bells. Golden *bells!*
> What a world of *happiness* their harmony *foretells!*
> EDGAR ALLEN POE

After the mothers have been seated, if the church has a bell, it is rung just before the wedding processional begins. Some brides choose to have the bells rung just before they enter on their father's arm. The church bell is rung again after the couple is pronounced man and wife.

HERE COMES THE BRIDE! THE WEDDING PROCESSIONAL

> The *bride* . . . floating all white *beside* her father
> Shadow of *trees*, her veil flowing with *laughter.*
> D. H. LAWRENCE

At the sound of the processional music, the mothers rise, followed by the congregation, and everyone turns to watch the processional. Also, the minister, followed by the bride-groom and the best man, enter from the side entrance of the church. When they reach their places that are often marked in chalk, they turn and face the aisle. The shortest usher, fol-lowed by the remainder of the ushers by graduating heights, begin walking down the aisle, or enter through the side, approximately four paces apart. If the wedding party is large, the usher/groomsmen may enter two at a time. Next come the bridesmaids, arranged by height, four paces apart; then the junior bridesmaids, the flower girl, the ring bearer, and finally, the bride and her father.

When my (Susan's) friends Sarah and Victor Kabutha were married, a flower girl preceded the bride strewing rose petals in her path. Sarah's mother explained to me that those weren't just ordinary rose petals, but those were petals that Sarah had plucked from the roses that Victor had sent her throughout their courtship. How charming! If your sweetheart sends you flowers, save those petals for your wedding day!

Collect them in a vase or bowl and they will dry out naturally. Add some rose-scented potpourri oil or another favorite fragrance to the petals.

FLOWERS FOR THE BRIDE AND BRIDEGROOM'S MOTHERS

When the bride's father escorts her down the aisle, they pause at her mother's pew so the bride can present a flower from her bouquet to her mother. At the close of the ceremony, the newlyweds pause at the bridegroom's mother's pew, where the bride gives her a flower, now that she is a new family member. Ask the florist to provide the mothers' favorite flowers or a flower they carried in their wedding bouquets.

THE BETROTHAL

When the bride approaches, she releases her father's arm as the groom steps forward to meet her. She transfers her flowers to her left hand, and gives her right hand to the groom to rest on his left arm. At this point in the ceremony, the minister signals the congregation to be seated. The father remains while the minister reads the betrothal, but when he asks, "Who giveth this woman in marriage," the father replies, "I do" or "Her mother and I." The bride gives her father a kiss, and he takes his seat.

Back in medieval times, brides were often captured by grooms from neighboring villages. After capture, she was kept at his left so he could keep his right hand or sword hand free to ward off any sudden attacks.

A FATHER'S BLESSING

My (Susan's) childhood friend, Cecilia Gunn Tinney, told me that when her daughters, Claire and Kate, were married, their father prayed a special blessing just before giving his girls away. What a touching and endearing gift from the father of the bride!

THE WEDDING VOWS

After the bride's father is seated, the minister leads the couple, accompanied by their honor attendants, flower girl, and ring bearer up to the altar. Or, in some churches, they may remain where they are standing. The bride gives her flowers to the maid of honor. The wedding vows are then spoken.

You can incorporate Scripture and your favorite poetry into the wedding vows. Customizing your vows not only personalizes your ceremony, but also is an inspiring way to make your wedding special. Some of the most widely used Scriptures are: 1 Corinthians, chapter 13; Ruth 1:16-17; and Ecclesiastes 4:9-12.

SPECIAL READINGS AND REMEMBRANCES

The couple often invites someone close to them to read one of the passages of Scripture or a special poem during the ceremony. If either of the couple's parents or a close family member is deceased, there are often moments of silence or words of remembrance to honor them during the ceremony.

THE DOUBLE RING CEREMONY

This *ring* is *round* and hath no end.
So is my *love* unto my *friend*.
SIXTEENTH CENTURY VERSE

The exchange of the rings—a symbol of love and commitment—is a solemn occasion. The best man hands the bride's ring to the minister, or is instructed to lay the ring on the clergy's open Bible. The maid of honor places the groom's ring on the Bible. The minister blesses the rings, and proceeds with the double ring ceremony. The bridegroom, reciting his ring vows, places the bride's ring on her finger first, and then the bride places the ring on her bridegroom's finger and repeats her vows.

COMMUNION

The minister may serve communion to the couple as a part of the wedding ceremony. The wedding party and the wedding guests may also partake of communion.

BLESSING AND PRAYER

After the couple exchanges rings, the minister says a blessing and a prayer, or sometimes a soloist will sing "The Lord's Prayer." If the couple kneels for the prayer, there should be a kneeling bench. The bridegroom helps his bride up after the prayer.

YOU MAY KISS THE BRIDE!

In ancient times, a kiss sealed a bargain; so at the time of betrothal, a ring was placed on the woman's finger, and a kiss was exchanged in front of witnesses. There were no broken engagements then! If the groom decided to back out after the kiss, he would have to forfeit all his possessions, and they became the property of the bride.

Today's kiss has a more romantic significance. When the minister pronounces the couple husband and wife, the groom lifts her veil and kisses his bride, but *Aunt Grace* suggests that you save those passionate kisses for the honeymoon. The maid of honor adjusts the bride's veil and train, and returns her flowers. The minister then introduces them to the congregation, as Mr. and Mrs. The bride and groom turn to walk back down the aisle.

THE RECESSIONAL

The ring bearer will escort the flower girl down the aisle behind the couple, followed by the maid of honor and best man. The usher/groomsmen will each escort a bridesmaid down the aisle. If there are more usher/groomsmen than bridesmaids, then they will descend two by two after the bridesmaids have departed. The minister remains in his place. When the wedding party has exited, two of the ushers return to escort the mothers back down the aisle, and then the grandmothers.

CHAPTER ELEVEN

Happily Ever After

THE RECEPTION AND HONEYMOON

❦

(Love) is perhaps the only *glimpse* we are permitted of *eternity*.

HELEN HAYES

THE RECEPTION

Following the wedding pictures, the bride and groom leave the church for the reception. If it is a short distance away, a walking procession is charming, or if the location is quite a distance, transportation is pre-arranged by the bride's family.

THE GUEST BOOK AND GIFT TABLE

The bride's family often provides drinks and refreshments, while the guests wait for the receiving line to form. Guests drop off their presents at the gift table, and then proceed to the guest book table that is usually covered with a white or colored cloth, often overlaid with tulle. The floral designer can arrange a bridesmaid's bouquet to decorate the table or attach boughs of flowers to the edge of the table.

At the top of each page of the guest book, the bride and groom can write sentimental trivia about their courtship—including how they met, favorite dates, a cherished poem, and other sentimental notes for the guests to enjoy. Some couples request that their guests pen some words of wisdom regarding marriage. Contemporary brides are replacing the guest book with a matted picture frame for the guests to sign. This artwork is later placed around a wedding photograph. Photos of the bride and groom and their families can be placed throughout the reception area. Wedding pictures of parents and grandparents are fun to see!

JUMPING THE BROOM

Jumping the broom originated with the onset of slavery in the United States when slaves were denied the right to marry in the eyes of the law. Being spiritual, the slaves created their own ceremony to prepare them for their jump *into family life. The bride and groom would gather before witnesses, pledge their devotion to each other, and end the ceremony by jumping the broom into matrimony. The broom was held about a foot off the ground while someone beat an African drum. This charming custom is often used in weddings today in honor of a couple's African-American heritage.*

THE RECEIVING LINE

The receiving line is optional, but it seems to be the most efficient way for the guests to greet the couple. If there is no line, the bride's father should be near the entrance to welcome and greet the guests. The members of the wedding party should mingle with the guests.

At large weddings, the bride will appoint someone to stand at the head of the receiving line. Each guest will give the announcer their name to be announced to the bride's mother. The order of the receiving line is as follows: Mother of the Bride, Father of the Bride, Mother of the Bridegroom, Father of the Bridegroom, Bride, Bridegroom, Maid of Honor, Matron of Honor, and Bridesmaids. The best man, ushers, and children do not stand in the receiving line.

A receiving line can be challenging when the parents are

divorced. While the couple should be sensitive to their parents, weddings should be a time when everyone puts aside their differences to honor the couple. Both parents should stand in the receiving line, if the couple wishes. The bride and groom's stepparents should mingle with the guests. If they are close to the couple, and no one objects, they can also stand in the receiving line.

SEATED DINNER RECEPTION

Engraved seating cards with table numbers are enclosed with the wedding invitation for formal, seated dinners. When cards are not enclosed, several assistants with seating charts can help seat the guests. These individuals are placed at tables divided into alphabetical sections. Seating assistants with lists are necessary, even when cards are enclosed, for those who may have left their cards behind. The tables are numbered and the seats are marked with place cards. Additional assistants should be present, to guide the guests to their table.

The bride and bridegroom are seated with their attendants at the bride's table. The bride is seated to the groom's right. The best man is seated to the right of the bride, and the maid of honor is seated to the left of the bridegroom. All the other attendants are seated at the table with their spouses or escorts. Additional tables may be needed for large wedding parties.

At the parents' table are the parents and grandparents of the bride and groom, as well as the clergy and his wife. Any other special relatives are seated at this table. The mother of the groom sits to the right of the bride's father, and the father of the groom is seated on the right of the mother of the bride.

WEDDING FAVORS

It has long been a wedding custom for the couple to give their guests favors. If the wedding reception is a seated dinner, the favors are placed at each guest's plate. Otherwise, the bride invites friends or children to carry baskets of the favors and distribute them.

Small silver engraved frames can double as place cards, and are great gifts to take home. Engraved silver bells make great gifts for the guests to ring when the couple runs to their get-away car, and then take the bells home. Packets of flower seeds for the guests to plant in their garden, potpourri, candy kisses, almonds, and candles are also lovely choices.

CREATE A TIME CAPSULE

Many couples are incorporating a time capsule as a part of their wedding reception festivities. The wedding guests are supplied with pen and paper and are asked to predict what the couple will be doing in the future, such as how many children they will have, what they will be doing, where they are living and anything else they would like to add. Save this capsule to open on your fifth, tenth, or twenty-fifth anniversary.

TOASTS

Let us toast to the *health* of the bride,
let us *toast* to the health of the groom,

Let us toast to the *person* that tied;
let us *toast* to every guest in the *room*.
ANONYMOUS

When the monk, Dom Perignon invented champagne in the 1600s, it immediately became a staple at weddings. Newlyweds can also be toasted with sparkling cider. The bride usually provides special toasting cups or flutes for the toast. The best man delivers the first toast, followed by the father of the bride, and then the father of the bridegroom. The groom may stand to add a few dear words about his new bride, while she remains seated. Ordinarily guests do not toast the couple, unless this has been previously arranged. Arrange to have a public address system for the toasts.

LET THEM EAT CAKE

It's *food* too fine for angels,
yet come, *take* and eat thy *fill*.
It's *heaven's* sugar cake.

EDWARD TAYLOR

Traditionally, wedding cakes were fruitcakes iced with white icing, but today they are white or occasionally, chocolate cakes with fruit or flavorful fillings, iced with white or butter-cream icings. Your caterer can provide the cake, or you may order from a baker. To save costs, your baker can provide a small decorative wedding cake, supplemented with large sheet cakes, to serve the guests. Only your bank account will know the difference!

Clip pictures of cakes from bridal magazines, or copy the cake from photographs of your parents' or grandparents' wedding. The baker will also provide pictures of cakes in his portfolio. Most wedding cakes are round, but some bakers offer unique shapes such as flowers, or my (Susan's) cake resembled a stack of wedding presents tied with ribbons.

TOP IT OFF!

Choose a special porcelain cake topper that you can keep as a treasured heirloom. Most brides choose a bride and groom that resemble them for the top of their cake. Your baker will have these available or you can purchase one at a specialty shop. Other choices are wedding bells, flowers, cupids, hearts, or lovebirds. A sentimental bride may use an heirloom cake topper, belonging to her mother or grandmother. Fresh flowers or a combination of fruit and flowers can also top the cake.

THE GROOM'S CAKE

The groom's cake is optional, but has become very popular at weddings. This chocolate cake is often topped with fruit-shaped marzipan; or can be whimsical in design, depicting a favorite hobby or the profession of the groom. We've seen football, golf, or movie cakes. Slices of the groom's cake can be individually boxed and given as wedding favors.

CAKE CHARMS

Four *tokens* must the *bride's* cake hold:
A silver *shilling* and a ring of *gold*,
A *crystal* charm good *luck* to symbol,
And for the *spinster's* hand, a *thimble*.
TRADITIONAL WEDDING RHYME

Before the wedding cake is cut, the bride gathers her bridesmaids around the cake to participate in a sweet, old-fashioned custom that is enjoying a revival among recent brides. When the cake is assembled, the baker places wedding charms attached to ribbons between one of the cake layers. Each charm has a special significance to the person who receives it. Each bridesmaid pulls a ribbon to discover her charm.

- Wishing Well . . . . Your wishes come true
- Heart . . . . Will find true love
- House . . . . Happy home
- Pineapple . . . . Home of hospitality
- Letter or Telephone . . . . Good news is coming
- Shamrock or Horseshoe . . . . Good luck
- Baby Carriage . . . . Blessed with children
- Silver Coin or Shilling . . . . . . Great wealth
- Engagement Ring . . . . Next to be engaged
- Wedding Bell or Ring . . . . . . Next to marry

CUTTING THE CAKE

Following the toasts, the cake is cut. Use your parents' or grandparents' cake knife, or a new one engraved with your wedding date. Decorate the handle with flowers and ribbons. Use it for years to come for anniversaries, birthdays, christenings, and other special occasions.

Before cutting, the top layer is removed, and wrapped for freezing, to enjoy on the occasion of the first anniversary. Invite the guests to gather around the bride and groom to cut the cake. The bride clasps the handle of the knife with her right hand, and the groom places his hand on hers. The bride cuts the first slice from the lowest tier of the cake, and gives her husband the first bite. In return, he gives her the next bite. This is a solemn ritual that symbolizes a shared life. Don't let *Aunt Grace* see you stuffing cake into one another's mouths!

Once the couple has fed the cake to one another, the remainder of the cake is cut by two servers and is served to the guests at their table, or the guests may pick up their cake from a serving table.

Individual cake boxes imprinted with the wedding date and the names of the bride and groom are popular favors. If the guests are unmarried, they are to place the cake in the box under their pillow to dream of *prince charming!* A boxed lunch of cake and other food served at the reception should be packed and sent along with the couple on their honeymoon.

TOSSING THE BOUQUET

Now *look*, ye pretty maidens, *standing* all a-row,
The one who *catches* this, the next *bouquet* shall throw.
TRADITIONAL WEDDING RHYME

Just before the bride changes into her going-away clothes for the honeymoon, she tosses her bouquet from a stairway, balcony, or raised platform to her unmarried bridesmaids and guests to see who will marry next! All single women are invited to participate. Ask your florist to make up a toss-away bouquet so you can preserve yours. This bouquet can be designed to separate into several mini-bouquets when tossed.

TOSSING THE GARTER

The groom gathers his unmarried friends around his bride, who is seated in a chair. The groom discreetly lifts the bride's dress and removes the garter. He then tosses it behind his back. The man who catches the garter is considered to be the next to marry. If the bride wishes to keep the garter as a keepsake, she may purchase an additional garter for the groom to toss. Modest brides who prefer not to lift their skirts can slide their garter down to their ankle or they may hand the garter to the groom.

CHANGING FOR THE HONEYMOON

The maid of honor accompanies the bride to the changing room to help her change. Often all the bridesmaids come along. The best man goes with the groom. Once the bride and groom have changed into their going-away clothes, the maid of honor and the best man notify their parents, so they can share some private moments before the couple embarks on their married life. Some parents like to present a special gift to their children—extra cash for the honeymoon, a piece of jewelry, a money clip, or wallet—at this time.

LEAVING THE RECEPTION

> Leave, *leave*, fair Bride, your *solitary* bed.
> No *more* shall you return to it *alone*!
> JOHN DONNE

Tulle or silk bags of rice, confetti, rose petals, paper rose petals, birdseed, or miniature bottles of bubbles tied with ribbons are handed out to the wedding guests, who are awaiting the bride and groom to emerge from their dressing rooms. Young people love handing out these goodies to the guests.

For a daytime departure, individual boxes filled with Monarch butterflies are a newer tradition and can be found in most bridal magazines. These exquisite butterflies are released just as the couple departs. What a beautiful sight to behold! Helium balloons tied with ribbons are another choice to release at a daytime wedding. Often the guests are supplied with pens or pencils to write a special wish for the couple on a piece of heart-shaped paper attached to the balloon.

For a sparkling send-off, provide sparklers or candles for the wedding guests. The guests can make an arch with their candles for the newlyweds to walk through as they depart. My (Ann's) brother Charles arranged for an elaborate fireworks show in the night sky for his daughter, Ashley's, wedding!

ROMANTIC DEPARTURES

Wouldn't every bride love to depart in a glass carriage as Princess Diana did? Recently, my friends (Susan) Marne Mink and John Halsey Woods, departed in a charming horse and carriage, decorated with flowers and ribbons attached to the horse's ears, signifying the knot was just tied. Our artist, Kathy Fincher, and her husband, Jeff, galloped away on their horses. My cousin (Susan's) Harriot Hall, described a formal wedding at the family's farm, where the couple left in a decorated vintage John Deere tractor! Other couples have sailed away into the sunset in hot air balloons, boats, helicopters, or small planes.

HONEYMOON HEAVEN

Moon, touch with shade the *bridal* doors
with *tender* gloom the roof, the *wall*,

And *breaking* let the splendor fall to *spangle*
all the *happy* shores by which *they* rest!

ALFRED, LORD TENNYSON

As you embark on your life together, phone both sets of parents the following day to express your gratitude for the lovely wedding. Although your wedding vacation cannot last forever, your honeymoon can.

CHAPTER TWELVE

The Second Time Around

SENSATIONAL SECOND MARRIAGES

⟡

The *heart* that loves is *always* young.
—GREEK PROVERB

Second marriages are becoming quite commonplace in our culture today because more than 50 percent of all marriages sadly end in divorce. When two people find happiness the second time around, especially after suffering broken dreams through divorce or death of a spouse, their wedding is a time of rejoicing and new beginnings. Here are some guidelines for helping plan that special second walk down the aisle.

PREMARITAL COUNSELING

Although they may have been married before, the couple should seek premarital counseling with their minister to be prepared emotionally and spiritually before making that second walk down the aisle.

THE PROPER THING TO DO

Following a divorce or the death of a spouse, it is advisable to wait at least one year before remarrying. Noted marriage psychologist, Dr. Neal Clark Warren, suggests that *all* couples should date a minimum of two years before they tie the knot. Only in rare circumstances does Dr. Warren approve of marrying before the two-year period, such as in the case of his father who was 92 years old! If the relationship passes this

test of time, the couple not only gets to know one another on a deeper level, but their relationship will be strengthened.

If only a short amount of time has passed since a divorce or death of a spouse, it is insensitive to expect children or other family members to rejoice if they are still grieving over the death of a marriage or a loved one. Remember that a wedding can be a very emotional time for the children of the bride and/or the groom. Prior to the wedding, the parent should explain to the child everything that will happen at the ceremony. The parents should appoint a close family member to care for the children and to be attentive to their needs throughout the wedding ceremony and reception since the couple is obviously very focused on each other and their guests. If a child balks about attending the second marriage of one of his parents, a counselor should be brought in to discuss the child's feelings.

SHOWERS AND PARTIES FOR THE SECOND-TIME BRIDE AND GROOM

Friends often want to host parties and showers for the couple to celebrate their marriage. Usually they choose a unique theme for the party based on the couple's needs. Couples who have been previously married should consolidate their household possessions to determine their needs and register their wish lists so their friends and families will know what they need.

A second-time bride always appreciates a lingerie shower. Coed showers also are very popular for second-time couples. Throw them a party with a theme with gifts for their garden, music, library, or movie videos. Try an entertainment shower, and give the couple tickets to movies, concerts, or buy them tickets to a play or baseball game. If the couple has children, a game or sports shower is a fun idea because the children can be included at the party. The entire family will enjoy these gifts of sports equipment such as croquet or badminton sets or board games.

CHOOSING YOUR WEDDING STYLE

There are really no rules about the size and style of a second wedding—it is strictly a matter of personal taste. If the bride-to-be eloped or had a small wedding the first time, she may want to have a large wedding with all the trimmings—whatever makes the bride and groom happy.

If the groom is marrying for a second time, and the bride has never been married, she may have any style or size wedding she pleases, as long as the proper amount of time has passed since the death or divorce of her bridegroom's former spouse. However, there are a few circumstances where a divorced man remarries a woman who has never married, that dictate a small discreet wedding.

INVITATIONS AND ANNOUNCEMENTS

Most second-time brides prefer the popular non-traditional invitations to the formal engraved ones. For small ceremonies, the bride may handwrite a note or telephone to invite the guests. There are many options available at your stationers for a second wedding. The couple may issue the invitation in their own names.

After the wedding, the couple can send announcements of their marriage to family, friends, and business associates.

THE GUEST LIST

The number of guests invited for a second wedding, like any wedding, is determined by the budget and personal preference. The couple may include family members, close friends, acquaintances, and business associates. If either or both, have children, it is thoughtful to invite a few of their close friends to share in the celebration.

Widowed couples desiring to invite their former in-laws, who are close to both you and your children, should speak with them privately to ascertain their feelings before you issue the invitation. Following a divorce, it is inappropriate to include former in-laws when you remarry.

WEDDING CEREMONY

You may choose to be married at home, a church, a small chapel, a hotel, or at an outdoor setting such as a beach, park or garden. Often, the couple will have a small intimate wedding at the church and then afterward, entertain their friends with a large party.

Talk with your minister about writing your wedding vows, or if you use the standard service, supply him with poetry or quotes to insert into the ceremony, making it personally yours. Have the minister tell your love story as a party of the ceremony. If you have children, write the vows to include them. A second marriage, where children are involved, should be a family celebration.

A bride is given away in marriage only once, so when she is married a second time, her father may escort her down the aisle, but the minister does not ask, "Who gives this woman in marriage?" Some second-time brides are escorted down the aisle by their children.

Many second time weddings include the unity candle in the ceremony, but instead of the parents lighting the two candles on each side at the beginning of the service, the bride lights the candle on the left and the groom lights the candle on the right. Following the ceremony, the couple will take their lighted candles and light the unity candle simultaneously. If either or both have children, they should be invited to light the unity candle with their parents to signify the blending of their families.

WEDDING ATTIRE

More and more second-time brides are having the wedding of their dreams, but we recommend that except for special situations, these brides forego a white wedding gown with a train or veil. They should consider a simple ivory or other color gown or suit. A hat with or without a small veil, flowers in the hair, or hair ornaments are preferable to a traditional veil.

For an informal ceremony, the bridegroom should wear a dark suit; for an afternoon wedding, a blazer and trousers or a linen suit; and for a formal wedding, he should wear formal attire.

When I (Susan) married, my young daughter Megan was my maid of honor and I allowed her to choose the bridesmaid dress she wanted to wear. Including your children in these decisions allows them to feel a part of the wedding.

ATTENDANTS

The number of wedding guests dictates the number of usher-groomsmen; one per 50 guests, or as many to escort the bridesmaids as needed. One honor attendant for the second-time bride is a good choice, unless the couple has more than one child, and then all the children should be allowed to participate as attendants, no matter what the number.

When one or both have been previously married and have children, it is of utmost importance to include all the children in the wedding ceremony. Young girls can be flower girls or junior bridesmaids and older girls can be bridesmaids or a maid of honor for their mother or future stepmother. If there are girls on both sides of the family, all the girls should be included. Sons can be ring bearers, usher-groomsmen, and the best man. Children of the bride and/or groom may light the candles.

Children may be asked to read a passage of Scripture or a poem as part of the wedding ceremony. They can also write a few words to say to their parents. The bride and/or bridegroom can read a special poem or Scripture to the children or with the children. The group may also recite a special prayer or poem together.

If the children are too shy to actively participate, their wishes should be considered. In those cases, they can distribute the wedding programs at the door, and at the reception they can pass baskets filled with bags of rice, rose petals, or birdseed. They can also help distribute favors to the wedding guests.

WITH THIS RING...*WE* DO WED!

Go *little* ring to that same *sweet*
That *hath* my heart in her *domain*.
GEOFFREY CHAUCER

One of the most charming rituals at a wedding is the ring ceremony. Following the ring ceremony, where the bride and groom exchange rings, the bridegroom then includes the children and presents them with rings, promising them to be a good husband to their mother and a good stepfather to the children. This is very special to bring the children into the ring vows. Silver rings with hearts, birthstone rings, or tiny gold signet rings with their initials are nice choices. Have the date of the wedding engraved inside the ring to make it a nice keepsake.

CHILDREN AT THE RECEPTION

Most second-time brides do not have a receiving line. The bride and groom should introduce the children at the reception. If dancing is included, following the dance with one another, the couple should dance with their children next. There should be some activities for the children at the wedding reception. Appoint a teenager to conduct games with the children.

Be sure to include kid-friendly foods at the reception. An ice cream sundae bar is a sweet addition to any family wedding. Ken and I (Susan) recently attended a reception where the waiters passed trays of miniature hamburgers. For a special dessert, serve cupcakes with miniature brides and grooms on top.

GIFTS FOR CHILDREN

Just as the bride and groom give their attendants presents for participating in the wedding, they should give their children special gifts. Suggestions for gifts for daughters are pearl necklaces, heart-shaped necklaces, bracelets, rings, and engraved silver or gold jewelry. Boys or girls would like watches, wallets, treasure boxes, or a Bible. Another idea is a gift for the family, such as bicycles, a trampoline, a computer or a television.

REMARRIAGE OF DIVORCED COUPLE

When a divorced couple reconciles and remarries, only the immediate family should attend, but the occasion should be a joyous time of healing. No invitations or announcements are sent. The good news is shared by word of mouth or personal notes sent after the remarriage.

GOING AWAY

When the bride and groom prepare to leave for their honeymoon, their children should have a private farewell with their mother and father. The adults who are caring for the children should come and get the children, and accompany them outside for the getaway. Children love to give gifts, so it is nice for the children to give their mother and father a special gift during this farewell time. An adult in the family should supervise the purchase of this gift.

THE HONEYMOON

Every couple should plan a honeymoon to get away. If you want to include the children, schedule a family honeymoon after the two of you have a few days alone together. A couple should telephone their parents and their children the morning after the honeymoon to express their gratitude.

Go now to your dwelling place,
to enter into your days of togetherness.
And may your days be good,
and long on the earth.

APACHE WEDDING BLESSING

May you live happily ever after!

Love,

Your Aunt Grace . . .

Susan and Ann

Acknowledgments

A heart full of gratitude to Barb Sherrill,
Shana Smith, LaRae Weikert, Carolyn McCready,
and all the Harvest House team!
A special thanks to Genevieve Smith.